HEROES

Heroes

STORIES OF SPORTS,
COURAGE AND CLASS

Ralph Wimbish

Charleston, SC
www.PalmettoPublishing.com

Heroes

First Edition

ISBN-13: 978-1-64990-726-4
ISBN-10: 1-64990-726-5

ABOUT THE COVER PHOTO

In February 1967, Rachel and Jackie Robinson came to St. Petersburg, Florida, to attend the NAACP's "Freedom Banquet." In the photo, they are flanked by the author's parents, C. Bette Wimbish and Dr. Ralph Wimbish, a past president of the local NAACP who led the fight against spring training segregation in the early 1960s. At far left is L.O. Williams, who was then the local NAACP president. Photo courtesy of the Tampa Bay Times.

Back cover photo: Ron Unternahrer

CONTENTS

Foreword

by Phil Mushnick

Several years ago, I was talking boyhood with Ralph Wimbish, the New York Post's former assistant sports editor. We're the same age, thus it stood to reason that we'd share many of the same memories. Turned out, we do and we don't.

I told Ralph that the first Black family I ever saw star in a TV commercial was Elston Howard's, in a Gulden's mustard ad in the early '60s that ran on WPIX Yankee telecasts.

Ralph recalled that, too, then calmly added, "Elston Howard used to stay in our home during spring training. He'd sleep in my room."

In 2001, "Elston and Me – The Story of the First Black Yankee" was published. It was authored by Howard's widow, Arlene, but researched and crafted by Wimbish. While there are a few mentions of the Wimbishes, their story is every bit as interesting. No, make that fascinating.

In the early 1950s, Ralph's father was a physician in segregated Tampa, then segregated St. Petersburg. Dr. Wimbish later became a regional president of the NAACP. Shortly before Ralph was born, in

1952, the Wimbish home, being built in Tampa, was destroyed by arsonists, believed to be Klansmen.

Dr. Wimbish built a new home in St. Petersburg that, in the late '50s and early '60s, would serve every spring as a haven for Black major leaguers whose white teammates were housed in segregated hotels.

"The Cards and Yanks trained in St. Pete, the Reds in Tampa and the Phils a few miles away, in Clearwater," Ralph said. "From the time I could remember, guests in our house were major leaguers. Bill White, Bob Gibson, Curt Flood and George Crowe, from the Cards. Sam Jones and Don Newcombe, at the end of his career, from the Reds. Wes Covington from the Phillies.

"Hector Lopez, when he became a Yankee, would be there. Minnie Minoso, with the Cards, too. He enrolled his sons in my school, Immaculate Conception, an all-Black Catholic grade school and we were in fourth grade together.

"It wasn't always baseball players. Jesse Owens, Althea Gibson, Cab Calloway. My house was a kind of clubhouse. They loved my mother's gumbo and my father, Bill White nicknamed him 'The Devil,' because he was always raising hell, filing lawsuits, leading protests and leading boycotts.

"St. Pete wasn't exactly like the deep South, it had vacationers and retirees from the North. But the theaters and restaurants were segregated. At Webb City, a department store, if you were Black and tried on clothes, you had to buy them.

"The white Yankees stayed at the Soreno Hotel, the Cards at the Vinoy. The Blacks stayed wherever they could. Curt Flood lived for a while in a room inside a garage.

"Elston was the only one to sleep in our home for any length of time. He'd use my room and I'd sleep in my sister's.

"I was only a kid, grammar school years. I didn't quite grasp why these people would stay with us. But I'd have dinner with the guys on my baseball cards, right there in my house. And my favorite player was sleeping in my bed. I thought it was great."

The front lawn at the Wimbish home served as the reception area. That's where the swimming pool was.

"The front yard, not the back yard, was where it all happened because the front was a lot larger. There was a law — a red line — that prohibited Blacks from living 100 feet from 15th Avenue South – the main road – and the front of our house was on that border."

Ralph's memories of another world remain vivid. He still has the visiting, gray Yankee wool uniform, Howard's No. 32, that Howard gave him when he was 8 years old. "I lived in it. I once asked Elston to come down the street to play ball with the neighborhood kids – and he did."

Bill White would take Ralph to Cards' exhibition games. "I might be the first Black to work as a major league batboy. April 2, 1964, Dodgers-Cards, Sandy Koufax against Ernie Broglio. Broglio won, 2-1. That year he was traded to the Cubs for Lou Brock."

Bob Gibson once baby-sat a 7-year-old Ralph at Al Lang Field. "I must've acted up, because in the clubhouse, he took me over his knee and spanked me. My father wasn't too happy with him about that."

In the summers, Ralph would visit his uncle in Harlem. The Howards would pick him up and take him to Yankee games.

Dr. Wimbish was a golf buddy of Jackie Robinson's. "I was in the Robinsons' den, in Connecticut, watching an Angels-Yankee game. When they got back from golf, Jackie switched to the Dodgers-Mets. I asked him to turn the Yankee game back on. My dad gave me a dirty look I'll never forget.

"Incidentally, my father was responsible for integrating St. Pete's public golf courses."

In 1961, partly because Dr. Wimbish refused to enable segregation any further by housing Black players or finding them homes, the Yanks moved to Ft. Lauderdale, where the players could stay in an integrated hotel.

Dr. Wimbish died of a heart attack, at 45, in 1967. Two years later, his wife, Bette, became the first African American elected to the St.

Petersburg City Council. She also served in Florida state government. After she died in 2009, the state named a major highway after her.

Ralph for years edited my columns for The Post. Now, nearly 60 years removed from his standing as the most popular kid on the block, he has many, many more tales to tell in this book. After all, they were the best of times, they were the worst of times.

The uniform top gifted by Elston Howard to an 8-year-old Ralph Wimbish was on display at the Florida Holocaust Museum's "Benches and Boycotts" exhibit that opened in 2019.

Introduction

Dave Anderson, the late, great Pulitzer-prize sports columnist for the New York Times, once told me about a simple way to know if you are a "real newspaper guy."

"Prick a finger," Dave said, "and you don't bleed blood. You bleed ink."

Well, I am a "real newspaper guy." For more than 40 years, I bled ink -- and sometimes profusely -- on the pages of some of the best daily newspapers in the country.

I was 16 years old in 1969 when I got my first journalistic transfusion at the St. Petersburg Times. I was a copyboy and I enjoyed hanging out in the sports department. It didn't take long before I got my first byline covering a high school basketball game. What a thrill it was (and still is) to see my name in 9-point bold-face type on top of a story I had written

When I went to college, I chose the University of South Florida in Tampa primarily because I could continue working part time at the Times. By the time I graduated USF in 1974 with a degree in American

Studies, I had enough clippings to land a job as a sportswriter for the Gannett Westchester papers in suburban New York.

There, I met some very talented people. I wrote stories about golf's Westchester Classic; I wrote about Jim Valvano when he got hired as basketball coach at Iona College; I covered basketball in Mount Vernon where I wrote about Lowes Moore, Scooter McCray and one of the country's top high school basketball programs.

In 1977, I took a job in suburban Detroit at the Oakland Press. I went to Tiger Stadium, wrote about the lowly Lions, had dinner with Minnesota Fats and covered one of Magic Johnson's first games at Michigan State.

Unfortunately, that job lasted only four months. That December, there was a bitter strike and I found myself walking a picket line in 10-degree weather.

It took me three months to get another job. In March 1978, I became a copy editor at the Post-Gazette in Pittsburgh, where I learned to design pages and watched the Pirates win the World Series in 1979. I also saw the Steelers win two Super Bowls and had my knee operated on — in the same hospital and on the same day as Dan Marino.

In 1982, I took a leave of absence and went to Europe, where I landed a job in Rome as news editor at an English-language newspaper called the Daily American. I was there only four months but I saw Italy win soccer's World Cup and nearly got blown up when my office building was bombed by terrorists.

I came home that fall to help my mother campaign for a seat in the Florida Legislature before taking a job as publicist for Golf Digest. For three years, I wrote press releases, helped conduct some tournaments -- including one for the "world's worst avid golfer" -- and edited an instruction book. But the "newspaper guy" in me got itchy and I eventually returned to the newsroom in 1986 as assistant sports editor at the Times Herald-Record in Middletown, New York.

In 1988, I landed my dream job at the New York Post. For 25 years, I did it all. I designed back pages, covered the Masters and two

World Cups, and authored weekly columns on NFL football, fantasy baseball and local golf. I edited Phil Mushnick and Peter Vecsey, won a car with a hole-in-one, played golf with Tiger Woods, wrote a book about Elston Howard, and wrote several feature articles for Dartmouth Alumni Magazine. I was also honored to be elected president of the Met Golf Writers Association.

By 2013, the daily newspaper business was in decline and I took a buyout. Since then, it has been very painful for me to watch as newspapers across the country fade away, cutting staff and news holes. Thanks to the internet, social media, viral pandemics and other economic issues, daily newspapers are fast becoming a treasured memory. What a shame.

And so, I am dedicating this book to the print industry and some of the extraordinary people I met and places that I wrote about over the past 40-plus years. People of class and courage who brought smiles to our faces and sometimes tears to our eyes.

I am also dedicating this book to my parents, Bette and Dr. Ralph Wimbish. Over the years, I had the opportunity to write about these two incredible individuals who raised me to be a sports-loving, independent-minded adult while they were under the stress of being at forefront in the fight for civil rights. They are my personal heroes.

For years, friends and family have been encouraging me to tell my stories. Well, here they are.

One thing, though. Please don't prick my finger. I still bleed ink.

Dr. Ralph Wimbish and his family in 1959: Ralph Jr., Barbara and Bette.
Courtesy Tampa Bay Times

CHAPTER 1

Batboy

My dad sat perched on the edge of his seat as Sandy Koufax fired the third strike. Another batter gone, John Roseboro, the catcher, flipped the ball down to third base as Koufax turned and reached for the resin bag. Kneeling on the on-deck circle, I knew it was now up to me. I had a job to do.

I was nervous, even if it was just a spring training game. I almost swallowed my gum as I pushed myself toward the batter's box. Crowd noise filled my ears as I reached for the bat. Deep inside I wanted to hit one out on Koufax, who was busy sizing up the next hitter. An intentional walk, maybe? No way, Koufax never had trouble with batboys.

I never got to swing at a Koufax fastball, but at least I can claim that, for one game in the spring of 1964, I was batboy for the St. Louis Cardinals, the future world champions. It was a day I'll never forget, if only because my dad was watching it as if it were a World Series game. Back in St. Petersburg, Florida, during the early 1960s, Dr. Ralph Wimbish led the fight against discrimination, and on this day, I was a part of that fight.

Before his death in 1967, my dad was the president of the local chapter of the NAACP. He organized several successful boycotts against local businesses that eventually helped integrate department stores, lunch counters, golf courses and movie theaters. But when Black ballplayers had trouble finding decent temporary hotel housing each spring because of hotel discrimination, he got angry and started another crusade.

It began when Elston Howard came to town for his first spring training camp in 1955. He soon found that St. Pete, a haven for winter tourists and retirees, offered no hotel rooms for Blacks. As more Black ballplayers joined the Yankees and Cardinals, the two teams that trained there each spring, the angrier my dad would get.

That's when my dad began to open doors, including the front door of our house. In those days, as I was becoming aware of racism, my dad would bring home an interesting lineup of athletes and entertainers and explained to me the ground rules of segregation. As I grew older, each spring would bring a different all-star lineup of house guests. We'd have Bill White in the kitchen, Curt Flood on the couch, George Crowe in the pool and Bob Gibson in the TV room. Wes Covington, who played for the Phillies, would come down from Clearwater.

My favorite house guest was Elston Howard, who actually slept in my room. I didn't mind getting exiled to my sister's room because I knew at school the following day I could brag that my favorite baseball player was using my bed. At the kitchen table I would show him his baseball card and read off his stats. Once, I got him to accompany me to the corner down the street where all my buds hung out. How great was that!

In addition to baseball players, other noteworthy houseguests included Althea Gibson (she slept in my room, too), Dizzy Gillespie and Jesse Owens. And there were a few "freedom riders" and Cab Calloway, too.

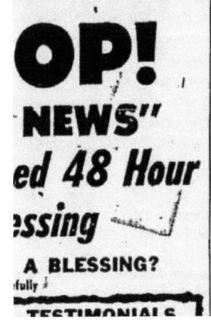

Doctor, police puzzled over cross burning

ST. PETERSBURG, Fla.—A six-foot, kerosene-soaked cross was planted and burned in the yard of Dr. Ralph M. Wimbish, 3217 15th Ave., South, here Wednesday night.

Police did not learn of the cross-burning until early Thursday morning although it happened Wednesday about 8:30 p.m.

According to police, a witness saw four men set the cross in the yard, light it and flee. The witness, a 14-year-old boy, said he told only his mother.

• • •

POLICE SAID Dr. Wimbish was away in nearby Tampa attending a meeting, and his wife, home alone, did not see the flaming cross.

Discovered by Otis Jackson, a caretaker for the doctor, the cross was brought to police headquarters and examined by Detective Dennis Quilligan. Only the tip of the crude cross was burned. The cross was examined for possible fingerprints but none was found.

Dr. Wimbish said he was at "a complete loss" as to why anyone would burn a cross in his yard.

• • •

QUILLIGAN SAID the affair might be the work of pranksters.

Dr. Wimbish, a native of this city, is an active civic leader. He is an outspoken opponent of segregation and led the fight to grant colored golfers the right to use city - operated course. He was also the first colored person to build in the section where he now lives.

Newspaper Article Dated June 5, 1956

A day I'd rather forget, however, was the time when, at age 7, I was spanked by Bob Gibson. My dad and were at a game when he left me in Gibson's care while he got called to the hospital. I guess I got a little carried away acting out in the Cardinals' clubhouse after the game and Gibson flipped me across his knee. Ouch!

In 1961, my dad made a big announcement. He would no longer facilitate spring training segregation by finding separate accommodations for Black ballplayers. The national press, notably Will Grimsley, devoted entire column about my dad. Sport Magazine sent a young writer named Alex Haley, later of Roots fame, to St. Pete to do a five-page spread.

An uncomfortable issue spread through the baseball world this winter when a quiet St. Petersburg physician shook the tradition of spring-training segregation. In January, before 1961 spring training began, the St. Petersburg Times reported that Dr. Ralph Wimbish had advised the Yankees and the Cardinals front offices that he and other prominent local Negroes would no longer find segregated lodgings for Negro players whose white teammates lived in two of the city's luxury hotels.

Dr. Wimbish, an NAACP official, called upon the Yankee and Cardinal front offices to spearhead an assault on such discrimination involving dozens of Negroes among the 13 big-league teams that train in Florida. The effects of Wimbish's statement grew by a chain reaction. -- Alex Haley, Sport Magazine

All this attention brought about a few death threats, obscene phone calls and hate mail.

By 1962, the Yankees decided not to force the issue. Instead, they moved their spring base to Fort Lauderdale. Meanwhile, a new National League team from New York was coming to St. Pete to replace the Yankees. I was told the Mets would come only if their Black players could be housed in the same building as their white teammates. That spring, the Mets has their hotel out on the beach at Treasure Island, about 15 miles from Al Lang Field, where the games were played.

The Cardinals stuck around. They were able to house all their players at the Outrigger Inn near the Skyway Bridge. That spring, I was in fourth grade sharing a classroom with Minnie Minoso's two sons, Guillermo and Orestes. Schoolwork became a major distraction before afternoon ballgames.

When Elston and the Yankees left town, Bill White became my favorite ballplayer. He also became one of my best friends. He often teased me about becoming a linebacker instead of a first baseman. Every weekend morning, he would stop by our house for breakfast, and afterward, drive me to the ballpark and he'd get me in for nothing. After a while, several of the kids who routinely hung around the players' entrance gate — not to mention the ballpark ushers — began to think Bill was my dad.

Thanks to Bill, I eventually got my big break — a chance to be batboy for a day. I was in sixth grade that day, April 2, 1964, and my school was on Easter break. The world-champion Dodgers were playing the Cardinals. On the way to the ballpark, Bill tipped me off that the team needed a batboy. He told me that it might be me.

My pay that day was only a few old baseballs, an old Bob Gibson glove and a broken Curt Flood bat, but not once did I think about complaining to my union. I had no uniform like most professional batboys get, only a new Cardinals hat from the equipment manager who was supposed to be my boss.

Being a batboy wasn't tough at all. Three hours before the game, I carried the bat rack and helmets out to the dugout and spent the next few hours mostly stargazing. On the field, I was invited to play in my first (and only) major league pepper game. An outfielder named Charlie James took a liking to me, grabbed a bat and called me over to scoop grounders with Ray Sadecki and Curt Flood. All this ballplayer-like activity went to my head, and minutes later, I was doing wind sprints on the warning track. I huffed and puffed until Charlie politely suggested I'd be better off running around the dugout.

Johnny Keane, the Cardinals' manager, was very cordial to me. I sat next to him during much of the game. Red Schoendienst, the third base coach, flipped me an old ball, tugged on my cap and gave me an instant lesson in the art of bat-boying: "After he drops the bat," he said, "pick it up."

Watching batting practice from behind the plate was fascinating. My biggest thrill came when Joe Schultz, a coach later of "Ball Four" fame, used me as his catcher for infield practice. As he whacked grounders, I fielded throws home, mostly from Bob Gibson, who for some reason was covering first base. The rest of the infield was Ken Boyer at third, Dal Maxvill at shortstop and Phil Gagliano at second. Schultz even let me fire one down to second, and believe me, it was good enough to have nailed Maury Wills!

Suddenly, it was game time. In those days starting pitchers warmed up near their team's on-deck circle, instead of the bullpen, while the public-address announcer read the lineups. I hated the Dodgers, yet there was Koufax just a few yards away. I wanted to go over and shake his hand, maybe get an autograph, but decided not to since today he was the enemy.

Koufax's mound opponent was Ernie Broglio. On this day he worked through the Dodgers lineup with ease. Whenever Koufax took the mound. I sprang into action. Based behind the on-deck circle, I retrieved bats, chased down foul balls and picked up batting helmets. Occasionally, the home-plate umpire would signal me to deliver some brand new baseballs.

Koufax was sharp, but Broglio was better and beat him, 2-1. Between batters, as I would rush to home plate to pick up a bat, I sometimes felt the adrenaline pumping. What if I sneaked a peek down at Schoendienst at third? Would I get the hit sign? Would Koufax pitch me tight?

It all didn't matter. In the sixth inning, I was chugging back to the dugout when I spotted my father in the stands, looking down proudly on me as if I had just homered. Looking back, I gave him a quick wave with one of the bats. My dad smiled and waved back. He knew how dreams can come true.

Curt Flood was a frequent visitor to the Wimbish home in the early 1960s.
Courtesy of Tampa Bay Times

CHAPTER 2

Curt Flood

When Curt Flood died in 1997, some of my childhood went with him. Curt will always be remembered as the player who challenged baseball's reserve clause. To me, though, he was the greatest center fielder to hang out at the house where I grew up.

I was five years old when Flood came to St. Petersburg in 1958 for his first spring training with the St. Louis Cardinals. Back then, Jim Crow laws prohibited Blacks from staying in the downtown hotels. That meant major league players like Flood, Bob Gibson, Bill White and Elston Howard had no choice but to find housing in Black neighborhoods.

St. Pete, to some, was one of the most segregated cities in Florida. When Jackie Robinson came to town in 1957 with the Dodgers, he was heckled without mercy. It is said somebody threw a black cat onto the field.

My dad, Dr. Ralph Wimbish, was an avid baseball fan who also was the local NAACP president. My dad lived to make a big fuss against segregation and on at least two occasions crosses were burned in our front yard.

Thankfully, my dad never wavered and took it upon himself to find accommodations for Black athletes and a few notable entertainers.

Sometimes it was a tiny apartment or a bedroom over a neighbor's garage. Sometimes it was my bedroom.

Yes, there were nights I was banished to my sister's room to make room for the likes of Cab Calloway, Althea Gibson and Elston Howard, and I didn't mind one bit. How often do you get your favorite ballplayer sleeping in your bed?

Being eight years old, I really didn't know who Cab Calloway was. To me, he was this man who always had a big smile on his face, especially at my mother's kitchen table. He always was joking around with me and on one occasion he took me to the ballpark for a spring-training game.

One time, though, we got in trouble with my mother, who had dropped me off at the ballpark after school. I ran into Cab and he insisted that he would bring me home. I thought I was doing my mom a favor, but when she came to pick me up, I wasn't at the ballpark.

Well, my mother blew a gasket. She had no clue that I had come home with Cab. We both got yelled at.

Our family had a swimming pool in our front yard and often I would come home from school to find players like Gibson, George Crowe, and White on the patio. Flood would often be in the kitchen talking with my mother.

"He loved southern cooking," my mom, Bette Wimbish, told me in 1997. "He was a real handyman in the kitchen, helping out."

Flood was a keen art lover and he took a strong interest in my mom's paintings.

"He had a great sense of youth," my mom said. "He had a great sense of patience, a great sense of direction, a sharp mind."

Curt even helped me break out of a Little League slump by giving me one of his bats. It had a little crack in it, but I put some tape on it and I began to have dreams of stardom.

Years later, Arlene Howard told me -- and my mother concurred -- about the time Flood had to hide in my closet. Apparently, he was having an affair with one of my mom's best friends and one day her husband found out. He came to our house with a gun, looking for Curt. Fortunately, Curt saw him coming and dashed into my bedroom.

Some nights, my dad would call up Flood, Gibson and White and take them out to local restaurants just to see if they could get served. That's one reason White labeled my dad as "The Devil."

In 1961, my dad put his foot down. He made a big announcement that was picked up by the national press (notably Will Grimsley of the Associated Press) that he would no longer help the Yankees and Cardinals – the two teams training in St. Pete that spring -- find housing for their Black ballplayers. My dad said it was time the local hotels had to open their doors. He also told the Cardinals and Yankees it was now up to them to force the issue.

The Yankees responded with the announcement that they would be moving their spring base to Fort Lauderdale starting in 1962. When August Busch, the Cardinals' owner, got wind of a possible boycott of his beer, he, too, threatened to find a new base.

That's when things began to change. The Cardinals soon found a hotel near the Skyway bridge that accommodated Black and white players.

Meanwhile, the local yacht club finally agreed to invite Black players to their big breakfast. Bill White said he wouldn't go, setting off a mild argument one evening in the Wimbish kitchen.

Simply put, Bill didn't want to get up early in the morning to eat with a bunch of racists. Flood sided with my mother and insisted Bill should go.

"Curt thought it was important to break down the barriers, make inroads so that Black ballplayers could be recognized," my mom recalled. "But Bill held firm and said no. He wouldn't go."

White never went to the yacht club breakfast. But the Cardinals stayed in St. Pete and won three National League pennants in the '60s, including the World Series in 1964 against the Yankees and in 1967 against the Boston Red Sox.

My dad died in 1967, so he wasn't around to see Flood lose his fight against baseball's dreaded reserve clause or Gibson become a dominant Hall of Fame pitcher or White become National League president.

I'm sure my dad was smiling down on them as it all happened.

CHAPTER 3

Jackie Robinson

The man who answered the door had a familiar smile, one that I recognized immediately from an old baseball card I had. Jackie Robinson, the man who had opened the doors of baseball for Blacks, was now opening his front door for me.

The year was 1964. My dad, Dr. Ralph Wimbish, a civil rights leader from St. Petersburg, had brought me, an 11-year-old Yankees fanatic, and the rest of our family to the Connecticut home of the Brooklyn Dodgers great for a weekend visit.

Jackie Robinson, I'm proud to say, was a friend of my father. As president of the St. Petersburg NAACP in the early 1960s, my dad led the fight against spring training segregation, and Jackie took notice.

And so, on this weekend in May 1964, two years after Jackie Robinson's induction into the Hall of Fame, my dad took our family to Jackie's house. Coming from Florida to New York City that Memorial Day weekend -- mainly to take in the World's Fair -- little did I realize how special this weekend visit would be.

It was already dark on that Friday when our car pulled up in front of the Robinson home outside of Stamford. My 3-year-old brother and I tumbled out of the backseat and we were soon shaking hands with "Mr. Robinson." He even laughed when I told him one of my best friends in school was named Jackie Robinson.

It was late, so Jackie's wife Rachel showed me the way to Jack Jr.'s bedroom. Mr. Robinson's son was about four years older than I, and he was away for the weekend.

The next day, while "Mr. Robinson" and my dad were playing golf, I spent much of the afternoon in the Robinson den, a wood-paneled room lined with old baseball and family photos and plaques. Yeah, that was impressive, but as a Yankee fan I was more interested in watching the Yankees- Angels on Channel 11 at the Stadium, a game the Yankees were winning until Bobby Knoop blasted a grand slam.

Late in the game, as I was awaiting a Yankee rally that never came, Mr. Robinson came into the room and made his way to his favorite chair. During a commercial break I went to the bathroom. When I came back, Mr. Robinson had switched to Channel 9 to watch the Dodgers play the Mets.

Hey! But, really, what could I say? I wanted to watch the Yankees, but I sat there restlessly until the next commercial. Mr. Robinson, sensing my uneasiness, offered to switch back to the Yankee game.

My dad, being the devil that he was, gave me one of those "I'm-gonna-kill-you" looks as he assured our host there was no need to watch the Yankees. But Mr. Robinson wouldn't hear it. He agreed to put up with the voice of Phil Rizzuto for one more inning.

Later, after the Yankees had been vanquished by the score of 9-5, we made our way back to Channel 9 and the Dodgers game. My dad and I listened as Mr. Robinson talked baseball. He seemed to be confident the Dodgers would be returning to the World Series that fall. They didn't, however, as the Cardinals won the World Series that year against the Yankees.

Dr. Ralph Wimbish introduces Jackie Robinson at the 1967 St. Petersburg NAACP Freedom Banquet. Courtesy of Tampa Bay Times

What I found particularly interesting was that Mr. Robinson could read pitches off the TV. Even with the TV camera positioned way up in the mezzanine behind home plate, he was able to distinguish if the pitch was a fastball, curve, or slider.

Watching baseball with Mr. Robinson was something I will never, ever forget. Sure, I'll never forget the trophies, the cookout, and the fireworks I shot off the night before we left.

But I don't remember if I thanked Jackie Robinson for his hospitality and, most of all, everything he did for my favorite game.

Thanks, Mr. Robinson. Thank you so much.

CHAPTER 4

My Dad

The events of 1967 continue to swirl about in my mind as if it were yesterday. It was an amazingly historic and unforgettable year – amazingly historic because of what my dad, Dr. Ralph M. Wimbish, accomplished and unforgettable for me because ... well, because I am his son.

Anyone familiar with the history of St. Petersburg, Florida, should know how important my parents, Ralph and Bette Wimbish, were in the local fight against segregation. Because of their efforts, restaurants, theaters, public restrooms, beaches, swimming pools, schools and hospitals had become integrated by 1967, the year my dad died of a heart attack at the age of 45.

To this day, I am convinced he might have lived longer if he hadn't spent much of his life fighting racism.

My dad was born in Cordele, Georgia, in 1922, and he and my grandmother Inez, a hotel elevator operator, moved to St. Pete in the late '20s. They lived on Third Avenue South in the Gas Plant district, a Black neighborhood that was torn down in the '80s to make way for Tropicana Field.

Dr. Ralph Wimbish, president of the St. Petersburg branch of the NAACP, integrates a lunch counter in the early 1960s. Courtesy of Tampa Bay Times

My grandfather Luther came with them but soon after divorced Inez and moved to Valdosta, Georgia. He remarried and his occupation in my dad's 1940 college application was listed as a barber.

My dad graduated from Gibbs High School and, after serving in the Army, then Florida A&M. On his college application, he wrote that his career ambition was to be a tailor.

At FAMU, he met a pretty coed named Bette Davis and they were formally married on Valentine's Day 1945, though they had secretly eloped in November of 1944 in Wilmington, Delaware. My mom was working as a riveter at a nearby Navy ship-building yard.

Sometime after my dad had graduated at the top of his class at Meharry Medical School in Nashville and completed an internship at Harlem Hospital in New York, my parents began building a house in Tampa on the "white side" of 22nd Street, across from the College Hill housing project.

Mysteriously, the house burned down in 1948 on the night before my family was to move in. My dad later told me he put the blame of the owner of a nearby store whom he suspected belonged to the Ku Klux Klan.

I am sure this was not the fire that burned deep inside my father as he began his crusade for civil rights.

Shortly after I was born in 1952, my dad decided to move his medical practice to St. Petersburg. Our family built another house on the north side of 15th Avenue South at 32nd Street. Because of rigid, but unofficial, zoning restrictions — the so-called red line— that barred Black people from living 100 yards of 15th Avenue, we had a big front yard.

Black entertainers and athletes who came to town could not stay in the city's segregated hotels, so my dad helped them find accommodations elsewhere. Our house guests included Cab Calloway, Elston Howard, Dizzy Gillespie, Althea Gibson, and Jesse Owens.

All this time, my dad campaigned vigorously against racial injustice. An imposing 6-foot pillar of testosterone with a mustache, he was a larger-than-life advocate of equal opportunities in health, housing, and education. He became the local NAACP president and organized a successful nine-month boycott of Webb's City, the giant downtown department store.

He drew national media attention for teaming up with Bill White, Bob Gibson, Curt Flood, and other Major League Baseball stars to end segregation that prevented Black players from staying in white hotels.

My dad founded the Ambassadors Club, an organization of Black professional men that became influential in many community-service projects before it disbanded in 2005. In addition, my dad filed lawsuit after lawsuit and attended countless county school board meetings, arguing vocally that Black schools and Black students were being shortchanged.

My mother, meanwhile, was no ordinary homemaker. While pregnant with my brother Terry, she courageously ran unsuccessfully for the county School Board in 1960. She also fed our family, drove her children to and from school and attended various community meetings. She also attended most of my baseball games when I integrated the Lake Maggiore Little League in 1964.

My mom entered college at age 16 and had heart set on becoming a doctor. When my dad was at med school, she took a job in Tampa as a junior high school teacher. In the early '60s, she wanted to attend Stetson Law School, not far from our home. But Stetson did not admit its first Black student until 1971.

Eventually, she was accepted at Florida A&M law school, and my parents made the tough decision to split up our family. With my sister, Barbara, already at Howard University, my brother and I went to Tallahassee with my mom in 1965 while my dad stayed home to support us.

I hated Tallahassee. I hated to leave St. Pete and spring training, my friends, and my schoolmates. Most of all, however, I missed my dad.

Usually, once a month and most holidays, we would make the 250-mile drive home, or my dad would come to Tallahassee. Still, we longed for the day until we again would be a normal family under one roof.

Because of that, my mom was determined to zip through law school in just 2 1/2 years, all the while attending to the needs of my brother and me. When the summer of 1967 arrived, she had just one semester to go to get her degree.

That summer of love was just that. It began with my sister's graduation from Howard and ended with her festive wedding reception in early September. In between, I worked for Charlotte McCoy at Doctors Pharmacy on 22nd Street. It wasn't my first job — I sold Cokes at Florida State football games the previous fall — but now I was earning $1.25 an hour as a stock clerk.

I played baseball that summer at Hoyt Field in Gulfport, and I smoked my first (and last) cigarette. Unlike years past, I could go to Biff Burger or Wolfie's restaurant in Central Plaza without having to use the back door.

When I got my learner's permit, my dad took me to a nearby parking lot to give me driving lessons. And there was golf. My passion for the game today wouldn't exist if my dad had not taught me to play at Airco, a local golf course he personally integrated. To some, he was St. Pete's version of Martin Luther King Jr. To me, he was my Earl Woods.

When summer ended, I talked my parents into letting me stay home to start my sophomore year of high school at Bishop Barry while my mom and brother returned to Tallahassee for the final three months.

That fall, my dad and I became closer than ever before. We played some golf and got to watch the final weekend of baseball's last great pennant race, when the Red Sox sneaked into the World Series. He loved baseball. In 1960 and 1961, he took me to New York for the World Series. We got our tickets courtesy of Elston Howard.

My dad was still a busy man, and I really began to appreciate the time he would spend with me, all the while his civil-rights activism and all those late-night house calls began to wear him down. Smoking two packs of Salems a day didn't help, either.

On the evening of December 1, my brother and mom flew to Miami to join us so we could attend FAMU's Orange Blossom football game the following night. I should have realized something was wrong that morning when my dad told me his tongue was bleeding.

Later that night, at the Four Ambassadors Hotel, I went to sleep about midnight, only to be awaken by the screams of my mother. Paralyzed by fear, I couldn't get out of bed. I heard the paramedics come and go before I mustered the courage to seek out my mother.

With no one to comfort her, she came running toward me. "I'm sorry, I'm sorry," she cried out, as if she needed to apologize. "I tried to save him. He had a heart attack. I'm sorry."

I never had seen my mother cry and, suddenly, I was in tears, too. My best friend, my dad, was in an ambulance speeding to a hospital, where he was pronounced dead on arrival.

Had he lived two more weeks, our family would have been at home, reunited again.

I stayed awake the rest of the night at the home of Dr. John Brown, one of my dad's best friends, thinking about a future without my dad. How would we survive?

Later that morning, my mother and brother boarded a plane home and prepared for the funeral. It still amazes me that my mother kept her composure throughout those awful days. Immediately after we buried my dad, she drove to Tallahassee and took her final law exams. Thankfully, she overcame her grief and passed them all and came home with a law degree.

"I did what I had to do," was all my mother would ever say.

Yes, she did. She certainly did.

CHAPTER 5

Chip Hilton

When I was 12 years old, the greatest athlete I had read about was not named Mickey, Wilt, Y.A. or Willie. His name was Chip.

Yes, Chip Hilton was a fictional athlete, but he was one of my favorites. Clair Bee, the legendary Hall of Fame college basketball coach, wrote 23 books about Chip and his triple-sport exploits. The first one, titled "Touchdown Pass," was published in 1948.

Back in the 1960s, before I discovered Sports Illustrated, The Sporting News and, yes, Playboy Magazine, it was fun reading about Chip as he played his way to stardom from high school to college.

My best pal, Daryl Stewart, and I spent hours in his room, each of us reading a different Chip Hilton book. It became a reading contest and the first to finish would slam his book on the floor. Once the reading was done, we would swap books.

Chip, who grew up in the mythical town of Valley Falls, could do it all despite all sorts of adversity along the way. He was Tom Brady, Christian Laettner and Cal Ripken rolled into one blond-haired, gray-eyed hero.

Chip Hilton was the hero in a series of sports novels written by legendary basketball coach Clair Bee.

Often, Chip would be placed in the position of getting his teammates to play up to his level and share his higher moral values. Occasionally his teams would lose but, more often than not, they won championships.

In the first book, there was tension between Chip and some of his "less fortunate" teammates from the other side of the tracks. By the final chapter, however, they had all become pals – especially after Chip saved the team's bruising fullback, Biggie Cohen, from drowning.

In one game, Central High was down by two points with 10 seconds to play. Chip was forced to scramble but could not find an open receiver. So, what did he do? He drop-kicked the game-winning field goal while on the run.

Hank Rockwell was Chip's coach at Central High and later at State College. Modeled after Bee himself, Hank was a stern taskmaster who always gave good advice and a firm handshake.

From Playoff Pitch -- Book 16: Rockwell's integrity and patient coaching methods had won the respect of the players. He had demonstrated that he believed in every player on the squad, on the field or on the bench. And he had demonstrated, so far in the games, that he wasn't afraid to use them in a game. Any of them.

One season, a new coach came to town and he let it be known immediately that his son was going to start at quarterback ahead of the more-talented Chip. With Chip on the bench the offense sputtered, but Chip kept winning games with great defensive plays. Eventually the coach, under pressure from his son who had become Chip's pal, had no choice but to play Chip at quarterback in the big game.

Then came a dreadful car accident. Central High had lost a heartbreaker on the road, and somehow Chip was left behind to hitch a ride back to town. He was picked up by a guy who had been drinking and the guy had a run-in with a truck that left Chip with a broken leg and a fear that his playing career had ended.

With his leg in a cast, Chip couldn't play basketball that season, but he provided inspiration from the bench as he cheered his teammates on to the state championship. By baseball season, Chip's leg was sound enough for his return to the mound. And, of course, Central High won another state championship.

From Clutch Hitter -- Book 4: Chip steadied his bat, holding it almost motionless. Corrigan took his stretch and then used all his height to drill an overhand fastball around Chip's wrists. Chip met the ball right on the nose, pulling it just a little. Before he dropped the bat, he knew he didn't have to run that one out. That one was over the fence, and the ballgame was good as over.

Chip's widowed mother, Mary, was a telephone operator and she was always there to lend support – especially since his dad, Big Chip, had died at the local pottery a few years before. Chip helped out by working part time at the Sugar Bowl, the local candy store.

Chip's best friend was Soapy Smith, a short, stocky red-headed kid who often provided comic relief. In football, he was a hard-nosed center who always made the big block. Soapy even managed to make the basketball team and win at least two games coming off the bench with his deadly, two-handed set shot from the corner.

Soapy was also a good catcher, calling some of Chip's best-pitched games. He also had the knack for starting a two-out rally or slugging a decisive home run.

From Hoop Crazy -- Book 5: Soapy banged a fist so hard on the fountain, it hurt. He resolved "startin' right now" to do his part to get the team back on track and to end the hard feelings between the guys.

Speed Morris was another interesting character. Chip's second-best friend was known for his quickness and drove about town in an old jalopy. In the football books, he was the scatback in Coach Rockwell's wing-T offense. In basketball, he was the point guard supreme. When it came to baseball, he was a sure-handed shortstop and a demon on the basepaths.

Speed was a great athlete, but Chip was just a little bit better. On several occasions there would be a race between the two. Speed would take the early lead, but Chip, with his long, graceful strides, would always beat him at the wire.

Speed, Soapy and Chip eventually graduated from Central High, and along with Coach Rockwell, continued their heroics at State College. Soapy even made State's basketball team as a walk-on.

Chip turned down a scholarship and got a part-time job as a stock clerk at State Drugs, where he met a potential girlfriend named Mitzi Savrill, the cashier.

From Backboard Fever -- Book 10: Mitzi was one of the top academic students in her class and also active in extracurricular campus activities and groups. Off campus, Mitzi wrote a column for the Herald, worked as a bookkeeper and head cashier and wrote short stories for young readers.

Soapy also worked at State Drugs and had a crush on Mitzi. But her eyes were on Chip, who was too busy being a hero to chase Mitzi or any other girls.

Clair Bee published his 23d Book– Hungry Hurler -- in 1966. The series sold over 21 million copies for Grosset & Dunlap, but the publisher let the books go out of print and they became collector items.

Bee died in 1983, but in the late 1990s, his books made a comeback in paperback. The Bee family gave permission to a religious publisher, Broadman and Holman, to update the series and make it more "politically correct." Chip's friends and teammates were more ethnically diverse — Speed Morris became Black, for instance— and Chip went to church regularly, owned a cat and did his homework on a computer.

In 2002, a 24th book, Fiery Fullback, was published after the Bee family uncovered an unpublished manuscript of Clair's. Now a senior quarterback, Chip leads his team to the Rose Bowl, but we were left hanging. Did Chip turn pro? Did he get drafted? Did he marry Mitzi?

A few years ago, I got a letter from Clair Bee Jr. He recalled the many hours his dad sat in front of an old manual Royal typewriter at their home in Roscoe, New York.

"He always had a No. 2 pencil in his mouth which he would bite down on when he ripped partially typed pages out of the typewriter, rolled them into a ball, and tossed them toward his trash can, which he usually missed," Clair Jr. wrote. "In my heart, [Chip) graduated from State and married his college sweetheart. The Vietnam conflict was brewing, and I am sure he volunteered and served as a faithful American, officer and gentleman.

"Chip was most assuredly a wonderful father and probably active in the Big Brother program. He would have stayed in touch with Soapy and Speed and must have had some wonderful reunions with them.

"With his God-given ability, he played well in the pros, and as his career as a pro player came to a close, he pursued a coaching career molded in the style — and love for the game and its players — as Coach Rockwell had so early in Chip's life instilled in a future All-America."

As for me, I tried but I was no Chip Hilton. I played touch football, some pickup basketball at the rec center and third base for various baseball and softball teams.

I was no star, but Chip's virtues are still with me to this very day.

CHAPTER 6

Tom Whelan

I worked with some very good and talented writers during my newspaper career. But there was nobody like Tommy Whelan. He wasn't just good; he was the best.

I met Tommy on August 9, 1974, my first day at work after being hired by the Gannett Westchester newspapers as a sportswriter – my first full-time job -- in their county bureau in White Plains. The day was particularly memorable because it was the day Richard Nixon resigned as president.

Guido Cribari, the longtime executive sports editor, welcomed me to the office that morning just as Nixon was leaving the White House in a helicopter. My first assignment, Guido said, was to join him for lunch at the Cane Pace media golf outing at Scarsdale Golf Club. As we were leaving the newsroom, we walked past a bunch of reporters gathered around a TV set and Guido barked out, "What's the score?"

When Guido and I arrived at the golf club, the first person I met was Charles Thomas Whelan. Here was a bald, 350-pound Irishman who if he had a white beard could have easily played Santa Claus at any department store.

Tim Whelan, mugging for the camera with Gannett Westchester staff artist Frank Becerra, was a walking encyclopedia of Westchester County sports.

Tommy was always jolly. He had a heart of gold and definitely a way with words. According to Tommy, New York's football Giants were "Mara Tech" or "Men of Mara." The crowds at Saratoga weren't fans, they were "parishioners." Bars weren't bars; they were "watering holes." And Yonkers Raceway was always "the venerable hilltop half-mile oval owned by the clan Rooney."

Nobody wrote like Tommy. His leads and stories were long, but each paragraph was packed meticulously with all sorts of information.

Big Towner, the Lee Broglio-trained, Lucien Fontaine-driven son of Gene Abbe-Tiny Wave who almost died a few months ago of an intestinal blockage, won his sixth straight start in eight tries since returning to action in April when he turned back the favored Governor Skipper in the first division of the Cane Pace. He was second in his other races. –Tom Whelan, 1977

Yep, Tommy was a loveable old-school scribe who began his career as sports editor of the Chappaqua Sun in 1955. Yep, he was a real newspaper guy and one of the kindest and funniest human beings you'd ever meet. He was inducted into the Westchester Sports Hall of Fame primarily because he was a walking sports encyclopedia. He knew just about everyone who played sports in the county. If you needed a contact, or the name of a washed-up boxer from New Rochelle who fought Rocky Graziano, all you had to do was call Tommy. He was a mentor to dozens of young writers, myself included.

"Tommy was my idol," said veteran New York sportswriter Rick Carpiniello, who worked with Tommy for more than 15 years starting in the late 1970s. "He knew more names than a phone book. He'd drive an editor nuts with a sentence that was 64 words long. But after you read it, then read it again, you were entertained. At least you read it again."

Chuck Stogel, a former Westchester sports editor who worked 18 years with Tommy, also has fond memories. "A day doesn't go by without thinking about him. If Tom Whelan was covering your high school game, that meant it was an important game. Tommy always walked the sidelines – he eschewed press boxes – in heat or cold or wind and rain, in a sport coat and tie, wearing a darkly colored shirt and no overcoat or hat. Known by just about every athletic director, coach and thousands of athletes over the years, it was extra special when Tommy was covering."

Tommy's favorite hangout was the bar at Sam's Gedney Way restaurant, where the drinks were always on him, and his favorite was Fleischmann's with water. When Tony the bartender would ask, "Whadda have?" Tommy would usually reply, "A repetition of the former." As he was getting off the barstool to make his exit, he would always recite the following checklist: "Spectacles, testicles, wallet, watch."

We worked for an afternoon paper, so Tommy would come to work around 11 p.m. or later, always in a jovial mood. Nobody cared he was late because he often showed up with a bunch of steak sandwiches for his fellow workers. Then he would nod off at his desk, which was across the aisle from mine.

When Tommy wasn't snoring, seemingly on the brink of falling out of his chair, he was at his manual typewriter, banging out long, complex sentences. He especially loved horse racing and had a column called The Clocker, which of course was his nickname.

Cormorant, a 3-year-old son of His Majesty, who ordinarily calls the Maryland circuit home, put all thoughts of unbeaten Triple Crown favorite Seattle Slew out of his head late Saturday afternoon and went out and won the seventh straight race of his career. The victory came in the 25th running of the Gotham Stakes by a widening 2 1/4 lengths over New York-bred Fratello Ed, a 17-1 shot in a surprisingly strong performance. —Tom Whelan, 1977

Early in 1975, I owned a green Ford Pinto that was always breaking down, leaving me with a mountain of car-repair bills that took a huge bite out of my salary of $150 (before taxes) a week. Financially, I was hurting but never hungry because every Wednesday, I enjoyed a big steak at Sam's restaurant courtesy of Con Edison, which sponsored a weekly media luncheon to pick Westchester County's top high school athlete.

The Wednesday after the Super Bowl, I arrived at Sam's restaurant, and Tony the bartender presented me with $300.

"Whoa!" I said. "Why am I getting this?"

"Congratulations, you won the Super Bowl pool," Tony replied.

Turned out, Tommy knew I was on the brink of bankruptcy and had bought me two boxes in the bar's Super Bowl pool without telling me. I couldn't believe it. I tipped Tony $20, gave him another $80 to cover Tommy's future bar tab and used the remaining $200 to pay off my creditors.

Thank you, Tommy!

A few months later, Tommy was responsible for my first visit to a horse track. Along with fellow writer Al Mari, we climbed into Tommy's clunky Oldsmobile 88 and went to Long Island to see a horse named Avatar win the Belmont Stakes. I had a dinner date that night and figured I would be home by 7:30. Boy, was I wrong.

After the race, Tommy and Al made a beeline to a rooftop cocktail party and there we stayed for the next three hours. There was no pay phone anywhere in sight, so I couldn't call my date to tell her I would be late. And besides, who was I to break up a good party?

Finally, about 10:30, the bar shut down and we were asked to leave. When we arrived on the ground floor, Al jumped out of the elevator and declared himself to be the fastest guy in our group, challenging anyone to race him around Belmont's mile and a half track.

Tommy and I declined, but three other guys accepted the challenge. Tommy took out his Clocker stopwatch and the race began. It took about a minute or two for the police to show up and put an end to the race. Fortunately, nobody was arrested.

Jimmy Roberts, long before he became a big-time sportscaster at ESPN and NBC Sports, worked as an intern with Tommy and me in the summer of 1975.

"Tommy wrote me the sweetest note," said Jimmy recalling his last day at work. "He gave me a bunch of silver dollars and said: 'Hopefully you'll take this and buy that cute girlfriend of yours a beer.' Of course, it was worded much more elegantly than that and in classic 'Whalenese.' A bunch of 'ahems' and such.

"This was my first job (in the media), and this was the type of man I got to look up to? Suffice it to say I would never encounter anybody as kind and decent in the business. What an incredibly sweet man."

Tommy also made a lasting impression on Carol Capobianco, a former New York Post colleague of mine who worked in Westchester with Tommy in the early 1980s.

"I was a new member of the sports staff," she recalled. "As a woman, I was a rarity in the male-dominated world of sports departments. The guys were going out for drinks. I walked to the parking lot a bit dejectedly, expecting to drive home — no one had invited me to come along. But there was Tommy in his car. He asked me if I wanted to join them at Sam's.

"He made me feel accepted, part of the team. The first of my colleagues to reach out to me on a social level. Tommy's kindness wasn't unique to me; it was his nature. He was sweet and jolly with a perpetual laugh. We need more Tommy Whelans in this world."

Another classic Tommy story involved the time he and Al Mari finished work on a Saturday at 6 a.m. and went to a nearby dive called the Valley Tavern to begin a drinking contest to see who could last longer.

According to Al, he matched Tommy shot for shot until about 8 o'clock that evening when Al realized he was about to pass out. So, Al called up his girlfriend because he wanted a dance partner to help him stay awake. She arrived, they pumped some quarters into the juke box and Al got his second wind. But sometime about midnight, it was Tommy who was about to pass out.

What do you do with a drowsy, 350-pound sportswriter who can't walk, much less drive a car?

It wasn't easy, but Al somehow managed to get Tommy to the parking lot and attempted to drive him home using two cars. Al would drive Tommy and his Oldsmobile about 200 yards or so, then walk back to his car to catch up. This went on for about 20 minutes until Al spotted a church and abandoned Tommy and his car in the parking lot.

Tommy said he awoke a few hours later to see parishioners in their Sunday best heading into church. "I thought I had died and gone to heaven," Tommy said.

Well, Tommy has been taking his last calls in heaven since December 29, 1992 at the age of 64. In his will, Tommy left $1,000 to Mike Taylor, his favorite desk editor, for a pair of parties to be held one year after his passing.

Those parties were duly held, with many "repetitions of the former" hoisted in loving memory of Tommy Whelan, our patron saint.

CHAPTER 7

Tiger Stadium

At one time, it sat majestically at The Corner -- Michigan and Trumbull -- in a rundown section of Detroit known as Corktown.

Today, not much remains on the site as that old, creepy dinosaur of a ballpark called Tiger Stadium has joined Ebbets Field and the Polo Grounds in that great ballpark heaven in the sky.

Of all the ballparks I have watched baseball, Tiger Stadium remains No. 1 on my top-five list, which includes Fenway Park, the old Yankee Stadium, Wrigley Field and the Polo Grounds.

The last game played in Tiger Stadium was in 1999 and the place was torn down in 2008, though it was the grandest of all baseball cathedrals.

Officially, the ballpark was known as Navin Field when it opened on April 20, 1912, the same day Fenway Park opened in Boston. Navin Field would have been front-page news in the Detroit Free-Press, but the big story of that time was the sinking of the Titanic a few days earlier.

"Baseball at The Corner," as broadcaster Ernie Harwell would say, was played there as early as 1896 when it was known as Bennett Park. In 1923, a second deck was added to the structure. In 1938, the northern end of the stadium in left field was enclosed and the place was renamed Briggs Stadium with a capacity of 58,000. The name changed again in 1961, this time to Tiger Stadium.

Joe Falls, the sports columnist for the Detroit Free-Press, was one of my favorite writers. Growing up in Florida, I loved reading his columns in The Sporting News about the Tigers and their ballpark. When I attended my first game there in 1977 as a sportswriter for the Oakland Press, it was a thrill for me to shake hands with one of my journalistic idols.

The place smells like a ballpark should," Joe often said.

Joe was right on. From the grandstand, you were so close, you could smell the green on the grass. At dimly lit concession stands, the red-hots smelled like hot dogs.

The ballpark was quirky. The upper deck in right field hung over the warning track. The dimensions were 440 to dead center, 325 and 310 down the lines.

Yeah, this joint had real charm, but it lost some of it in 1980 when a new owner came along and replaced the green seats with blue ones. Then he did the unthinkable: Bo Schembechler, the old University of Michigan football coach, was hired as team president — and one of the first things he did in 1991 was fire Harwell, the team's longtime radio voice. There was such an uproar, so much so they had to him bring back in 1993.

Ernie, who had personally welcomed me to Tiger Stadium press box, made the move to the new Comerica Park in 2000 and called his last Tigers game in 2003. He died at the age of 92 in 2010.

Many of the greats of the game made Tiger Stadium their home. Ty Cobb, Hank Greenberg, Mickey Cochrane, Sam Crawford, Charlie Gehringer, Harry Heilmann, George Kell, Hal Newhouser and Al Kaline went to the Hall of Fame. Denny McLain went to jail.

Kirk Gibson homered there off Goose Gossage in the 1984 World Series, Norm Cash, ever smiling, played first base with Kaline over his shoulder in right field. Ron LeFlore was always stealing bases. Hank Aguirre staked his claim as the worst-hitting pitcher of all time.

Don Mossi, with his big ears, played there, too, along with the likes of Mickey Lolich, Gates Brown, Willie Horton, Joe Sparks, Jason Thompson, Allan Trammell, Rusty Staub and Jack Morris. Even Walt Terrell.

And, of course, we can't forget Mark "The Bird" Fidrych, who talked to the baseball and won 19 games in 1976, including a classic game over Billy Martin's Yankees on ABC "Monday Night Baseball." The gawky right-hander, who rubbed the mound and shook hands with his fielders, was on his way to stardom until he hurt his arm in 1977 and soon after retired to his farm in Massachusetts. He died in 2009.

On June 24, 1962, the Yankees were playing in Detroit and I was in New York visiting my Uncle Alex in Harlem. Frank Lary, the grand poobah of Yankee killers, started for Detroit. I watched the first nine innings on TV before our family went out for dinner with the score tied at 7-7. And so I didn't see Jack Reed's homer win it for the Yankees in the 22nd inning.

Yogi Berra, who caught all 22 innings that day, loved the place. "It's a good ballpark for left-handed hitters," he told me in 1999. "You could see the ball very well, but the clubhouse was the worst. Too cramped."

From 1938 till 1974, the stadium was the home field of the NFL's Lions. Years later, before it was finally torn down, Billy Crystal had it disguised as Yankee Stadium when he filmed the HBO movie "61."

Three All-Star Games were played here with lots of home runs. In 1971, Reggie Jackson came to the plate against Dock Ellis and crushed one off the light tower way up in right field.

Six years later, on August 17, 1977, I was assigned to cover my first game at Tiger Stadium. The Tigers were playing the Yankees that night. Bill Stieg, a fellow sportswriter who would become one of my best friends, was there, too, and we got there early to watch batting practice behind the batting cage.

Elston Howard spotted me right away and we exchanged updates about our families. It was the last time we talked. Three years later, he died from a heart condition. Little did I realize that 20 years later, in 1997, I would begin writing his biography.

Suddenly, Bill and I looked up to see Thurman Munson come to the plate for batting practice, with Jackson awaiting his turn.

"I tell you, man, it was the most awesome home run I've ever seen," Munson said in between swings to teammates Fred Stanley and Cliff Johnson.

"Ah, gee. C'mon, Thurm," Reggie gushed, pretending to be embarrassed.

Johnson pretended he didn't believe a word Munson had said. "Naw, no way," he roared back.

"I was here. I saw it," Munson insisted. "It was awesome."

Yep, just like Tiger Stadium.

CHAPTER 8

Minnesota Fats

Minnesota Fats said he was hungry – very hungry -- as he took a seat in the far corner of the Main Event restaurant overlooking the empty seats of the Pontiac Silverdome.

"You know, this here is a nice place," he told me on the evening of November 2, 1977, when I was assigned by my newspaper to have dinner with the self-proclaimed "world's greatest pool player."

"I played two years ago in the Astrodome," he said, "and I was supposed to play Raquel Welch a couple of months ago in that place they have down in New Orleans."

"The Superdome?" I said.

"Yeah," he said, "that's it."

Rudolf "Rudy" Wanderone Jr. -- the name Fats was given by his Swiss emigrant parents -- was in town for a series of exhibition matches benefitting the Easter Seal Society Fund for the handicapped.

Fats, who claimed to be 64 years old, was to draw more than 300 admirers into the adjoining banquet room, where he would play pool against all comers – as long as they came up with a $50 donation. But before getting down to the business at hand, Fats wanted to partake in the only two activities he loved more than pool — eating and talking about himself.

"I want no steak," he said, grabbing the menu. "I've been eating them for weeks."

The waitress – who had no idea who Fats was -- arrived to take his order.

"Do you have fried shrimp?" Fats bellowed. "How about some cream of mushroom soup? And a heart of lettuce with thousand island dressing."

Fats then turned to me and said, "There's no food I haven't eaten. I've eaten all over the world. I've eaten with Arab kings. No living creature on earth has traveled as much as I have or done as much as I did."

Grabbing a dinner roll, he said, "I just got finished playing an exhibition at the Waldorf in New York. Ten days and nights could pass and I wouldn't know that I had been awake."

Minnesota Fats' plate was always loaded with charisma — with a bunch of bull on the side. Kids who never have seen him hold a billiards stick would cuddle up next to him and timidly ask for autographs. He has signed so many, he carried a rubber stamp.

Anyone who saw Jackie Gleason portray him in the movie "The Hustler" surely knows who he is. According to Fats, his value to the game of pool is comparable to that of Arnold Palmer's to golf.

"Look at tennis," Fats said between sips of iced tea. "It was a joke until Bobby Riggs came along. I'm the world's greatest pool player and wherever I go, there's publicity.

"Until Gleason did me up in the movie, pool was at its lowest ebb. But I began to back the movie up with appearances and now pool is the largest industry in the country."

Fats began attacking his soup. "There used to be 2 1/2 million pool tables in this country and today there's 16 million," he said. "People have found out what a fantastic toy it really is."

Fats grew up on Manhattan's Upper East Side, where he claims to have become a pool-hall regular by the age of 2.

By the time he was 10, he was nicknamed "Double Smarts Fats" because of his hustling ability at cards as well as pool. He says he became known as "Triple Smart Fats" and other colorful nicknames by the time he was 12 and went on a world tour as a billiards boy wonder.

After "The Hustler" hit the movie theaters in 1961, he stopped calling himself "New York Fats" and acquired the title "Minnesota Fats" because, as he puts it, "I broke everyone in the state of Minnesota."

Fats began eating his salad. "I can beat any pool player I want," he said. "Professional players, they're all queens for a day because I'm the best. I'm a total winner. I don't book losers. Nothing I do ever loses."

The tag "Fats" was an apt description of him until 1972. At 5-foot-6, he weighed more than 280 pounds then, but on this day he claimed to tip the scales at 210.

"I'm in as good of shape as you can get," Fats said before ordering a cup of coffee without dessert. "I don't drink. I don't smoke. I just eat a lot. The only drink I would have would be one of those 'Pink Squirrels' with lots of ice cream."

Fats was finished eating but he wasn't done talking. He bragged some more about his line of billiard equipment, his travels, his exhibition matches and his syndicated television show called "Celebrity Billiards."

"My idea of a vacation," he said, "is what I'm doing now. I like to keep pace, but people keep calling and calling and never leave me alone. I don't care. Nothing ever bothers me. That's for suckers."

Over the years, Fats kept hustling, taking on all "suckers" until January 15, 1996. That's the day he lost out to his heart at the age of 82.

His tombstone reads, "Beat every living creature on Earth. St. Peter, rack 'em up."

CHAPTER 9

Dick Enberg

Long before his voice became a soundtrack for TV sports, little Ricky Enberg was the best sandlot play-by-play announcer in Armada, Michigan.

Oh, my! Little Ricky dreamed about becoming a baseball player, so he would grab a bat and a bunch of tennis balls and head to a nearby ball field. As he would take his cuts, little Ricky would do play-by-play accounts of each swing and recite the Detroit Tigers' lineup just the way his idol, Van Patrick, had done on the radio the night before.

Little Ricky never made it to the majors, but he did become Dick Enberg, one of TV's all-time great sports broadcasters. Oh, my!

In 1952, the smooth-talking Enberg enrolled at Central Michigan University and played on the baseball team. But it didn't take him long to trade in his bat and glove for a microphone.

Enberg got his first break at a radio station in Mount Pleasant, Michigan, where he earned a dollar an hour sweeping the floor. As good as he was with a broom, station management quickly realized he was better reading commercials and broadcasting games.

"I really needed the money," Enberg told me in 1977 when I interviewed him for a story in the Oakland Press. "At the time I was just a farm-boy kid and nobody was directing me. Until I got that radio job, I would hitchhike to town to watch the (Detroit) Lions and Tigers.

"I remember one particular moment that I got so excited I wet my pants. We'd always wait for ballplayers outside the park and we would follow them. Ted Williams was my all-time hero and one day I followed him to the players' entrance. And Al Kaline and I were both the same age and I used to fantasize that he was me."

Upon graduating from Central Michigan in 1957 with a degree in health science and a minor in speech, Enberg moved on to Indiana University as a teaching assistant. He earned his health science doctorate in Bloomington while he was doing play-by-play for the Hoosiers' sports network.

In 1961, Enberg moved to California and became the baseball coach and an assistant professor at San Fernando Valley State College, a school now known as Cal State Northridge.

"I've always thought my background as a teacher separates me from other announcers," Enberg said. "The teaching gave me focus. If you can face 50 motivated students in a classroom, then to face a cold camera ought to be easy. I enjoyed teaching very much. Maybe someday I'll go back to it."

He didn't.

"I'm always drawing upon my experience as a listener of music, or history, sociology, or it might even be poetry," he said. "Anybody can talk about a ball or a strike, but it's what you say around those things that distinguish you as an announcer."

Enberg's voice was heard coast to coast in 1968 when he did the play-by-play (Bob Pettit provided the color) for the UCLA-Houston basketball "Game of the Century" at Houston's Astrodome.

Lew Alcindor against Elvin Hayes. Oh, my!

"That will always be memorable," he said. "That was my first national event. TVS (sports network) didn't know Dick Enberg from

Freddie Fungo. Of course, it was the largest crowd ever to watch a basketball game and apparently it really opened the door for the televising of college basketball."

In the 1970s, Enberg became the voice of college basketball. In addition to UCLA games, he teamed up with Al McGuire and Billy Packer to do games for NBC. He was at the mike when Magic Johnson and Michigan State defeated Larry Bird and Indiana State in the landmark 1979 NCAA championship game.

Enberg also did games for California Angels and the Los Angeles Rams.

Oh, my! By the mid-1980s, he was everywhere. In addition to weekly NFL and baseball's Game of the Week, he did the Rose Bowl, the U.S. Opens in golf and tennis, Wimbledon, the Masters, boxing and the Olympic Games. He even appeared in movies like the original Rollerball (1975) and the Leslie Nielsen farce, The Naked Gun (1988). He also found time to host game shows like "Sports Challenge" and "Three for the Money."

"When people ask me what sport I enjoy doing most, my answer is that they're all like beautiful women. You love each for their individual beauty," he said. "I like basketball because it's fast-paced and it gets me back to a college campus and with college kids. Football is the best dramatically constructed game of them all, while baseball is by far the most difficult (to play)."

Dick's voice and trademark phrase are no longer with us. He died of a heart attack in 2017 at the age of 82.

Oh, my! We do miss him.

CHAPTER 10

Magic Johnson

Blood was dripping from the side of Greg Kelser's left eye as he glanced over toward Earvin Johnson. The two exchanged satisfied smiles as they sat in the Michigan State locker room, cooling off after putting on a dazzling display of basketball in a surprisingly easy 103-74 victory over the University of Detroit.

"Earvin's passing was super, just as always," said Kelser, a 6-foot-7 junior who personified the role of power forward with 36 points and 10 rebounds as he and Johnson wowed a sell-out crowd of 10,316 at Detroit's Calihan Hall.

The game, a bruising affair played on December 21, 1977, was a harbinger of things to come for the heralded 6-foot-8 freshman guard from Lansing known as "Magic." He scored only 11 points that night, but it was his 13 jaw-dropping assists that had the crowd oohing and aahing.

"I love passing off. That's my job," said Johnson, averaging just 12 points after seven games. "When my man is open under the basket, I can't pass him up. If we need more points, then I might think about shooting more."

Magic took only one shot -- a slam dunk -- in the first half. His second shot -- a basket on a fast-break layup -- didn't come until there were five minutes left in the game and gave the green-clad Spartans an 81-57 lead over the shell-shocked Titans.

"Earvin and Jay (Vincent) are the best freshmen in the country, and I want you to quote me," Kelser told me and the other reporters. "They're blending their talents with the rest of us, just like we're blending ours with theirs."

With the victory, the unranked Spartans improved their record to 6-1; that loss coming 18 days earlier at Syracuse.

In 2017, when I was working on writing "Throw The Ball High," the Mickey Crowley book, I asked Dick Vitale if he remembered that game. "Yeah, that was the start of showtime, baby," he said. "They wiped us out. It was Magic being Magic."

Vitale surprisingly had stepped down as Detroit's head coach before the season after taking the Titans into the second round of the 32-team NCAA tournament with a 25-4 record. In fact, he was introduced to the crowd before the game and did a victory lap around the court, shaking hands with all the writers on press row, including me, covering the game for the Oakland Press.

Detroit, which trailed 39-32 at halftime, came into the game ranked 15th in the country with a 6-0 record. Led by John Long, Terry Tyler and Terry Duerod, the Titans went on to post a 25-4 record that season. But on this particular night, they committed 22 turnovers and were overwhelmed by State's zone defense.

Long, Detroit's top scorer whose elbow inflicted Kelser's cut eye early on, had a bad night, scoring just 13 points on 4-for-15 shooting. Tyler, a 6-foot-7 jumping jack, was stifled inside by Vincent and finished with 12 points. Duerod, a speed demon of a point guard, had 16 points.

"We couldn't get the key basket to get us rolling. We weren't putting the ball in the basket," said Detroit rookie coach Dave "Smokey" Gaines after the game. "Our players took the loss hard. I saw some tears in some of their eyes. That's the way it should be."

Swingman Bob Chapman has a good night, finishing with 22 points. Jud Heathcote, the Michigan State coach who was a maniac on the sidelines, was a little more jubilant. He said his team "came ready to play."

"I figured we'd win by one point, or if we were lucky, by five or six," Heathcote said. "I don't know if we belong in the rankings, but maybe so if we keep playing like we are and improving."

The Spartans went 25-4 and finished the season ranked No. 4. They won the Big Ten title with a 15-3 conference record and made it to the NCAA's Sweet 16, where they were beaten by Kentucky, the eventual NCAA champion. One year later, they won it all, beating Larry Bird and Indiana State in the 1979 final.

Johnson averaged 17.1 points, 7.9 assists, and 7.6 rebounds a game in his two years at Michigan State. He then played 13 seasons with Lakers, with whom he won five NBA titles.

Kelser played six seasons with four teams in the NBA. He went on to be a TV sports announcer and does Pistons game for Fox Sports.

Tyler went on to play 11 seasons in the NBA while Long played for four NBA teams. Duerod played five pro seasons and won an NBA title in 1981 with the Boston Celtics. All three had their collegiate uniform numbers retired by the school now known as Detroit Mercy.

Vitale went to the NBA in 1978 as head coach of the Detroit Pistons. Fired the following season after a 4-8 start, he soon landed at ESPN and became its top college basketball analyst.

As for me, that Michigan State-Detroit game was the last one I covered for the Oakland Press. One week later, the Newspaper Guild declared a strike that was never settled, and I was out of a job.

But not before I got to see the magic that was Earvin Johnson.

CHAPTER 11

On Strike

Believe me, there aren't too many things in life more miserable than walking a picket line for six hours a day in freezing weather. I spent the first two months of 1978 doing just that, and I can tell you it was no place for a 25-year-old sportswriter like me.

The Newspaper Guild, of which I was a proud union member, went on strike at the Oakland Press on December 29, 1977, a mere 4 1/2 months after I had started work at the suburban daily newspaper with a circulation of about 80,000. Our newsroom was in Pontiac, Michigan, home of the stadium that became known as the Silverdome, about 25 miles north of downtown Detroit.

It had been about two years since the newspaper and the Guild had agreed on a contract. When I was hired that August, I was getting about $300 a week and was told a "new contract" was on the horizon and, surely, I would see a raise in pay.

So, it was a shock that morning when Jim Grinelli, a veteran city side reporter with whom I shared an apartment, slammed down the phone and told me the Guild had called a strike, following the lead of the pressman's union.

My first thought was to check with my fellow sports staffers. Bruno Kearns, our sports editor, was management, but I think he was secretly in our corner. Fletcher Spears, his top assistant, was a hawk, as were my fellow writers Jack O'Connell and Bill Stieg.

Who was I to cross a picket line? I figured the strike would last a week, we'd get a new contract and I would get a decent raise. Boy, was I wrong.

When I agreed to the walkout that evening, I knew I had an ace up my sleeve -- a job interview the following week at the Daily News in New York City. So, after one day on the picket line, I drove to New York just before New Year's Eve.

At the Daily News, I was interviewed by sports editor Paul Durkin. I think Durkin liked me because he offered me a one-week tryout on the sports desk to begin the following week.

So, I headed back to Michigan, heard there was no progress on the strike, and drove back to New York for my tryout. I had some experience doing layout and writing headlines, but now I had to step up my game. This was the Big Apple. I really wanted this job.

One of the first headlines I wrote was a classic. The Cincinnati Reds needed permission from baseball commissioner Bowie Kuhn to make a trade for Oakland pitcher Vida Blue. My one-column headline read:

Reds need
green light
for Blue deal

"Hey, I can do this," I said to myself. Then a few days later, a disgruntled desk guy quit because he thought he should be covering the Mets. When Durkin asked me to stay another week, I jumped at the chance.

That following week it became apparent to me that working on the desk was a lot better than writing stories on deadline. I liked desk work.

I liked editing other writers' stories and writing headlines. Eventually, I also learned how to design individual pages. This was to become my true calling.

Unfortunately, no job offer was coming my way. I was told by Durkin I needed a "little more seasoning." So, I collected my second paycheck -- I was getting $150 a day -- and drove back to Michigan, which was being slammed by a blizzard.

Back in Pontiac, I took my place on the icy picket line, earning a mere $60 a week in strike benefits. Most of my shifts were 3 p.m. to 9 p.m., meaning I spent six hours each day walking back and forth carrying a picket sign on the sidewalk in front of the Press building. Often, I would gaze at a nearby time-and-temperature clock to see how cold it was and how much time I had left to be miserable.

Then came the time when I was nearly beat up by company goons. It was close to 8 p.m. on a Friday and I was alone on the picket line while Grinelli, my partner that evening, went over on a break to warm up at our strike headquarters. Suddenly a car load of drunk Wackenhut security guards pulled up next to me.

"Strike against the Press? We're gonna beat your bleeping ass," was all I heard as I dropped my picket sign and dashed across the street toward the safety of strike headquarters. Crossing Huron Street, I was nearly hit by a car.

Grinelli locked the door behind me after I rushed in and he called the police. Two officers showed up about 25 minutes later, but only after Grinelli and I braved another round of picketing. Again, the car full of goons pulled up and we hastily retreated to headquarters.

The next day, I began sending out my resume to a bunch of newspapers. I got replies from papers in East St. Louis and West Palm Beach, but no job offers. For meals, I joined a food co-op run by Jack O'Connell's wife Mary Ann, who made us some delicious dinners every night for $15 a week.

On Fridays, I took a part-time job as a pressman at the Detroit News. My job as a "flyboy" was to sit and watch the papers come off the press. If some papers fell on the floor, I was responsible for picking them up and throwing them away. I earned $8 an hour for doing that.

One day, I got a phone call from John Craig, editor of the Post-Gazette in Pittsburgh, asking me to come for an interview. On Monday, March 6, I drove to Pittsburgh and left my car, a Pontiac Sunbird, at a parking lot just up the street from the Post-Gazette office.

Craig asked me stay two more days for a tryout on the sports desk. I said OK, even though I didn't bring any extra clothing with me. Later that evening, when I got to my car, the driver-side door was all smashed up. I was told one of the parking-lot attendants had moved my car onto the street and opened my car door just as a truck was passing by.

The parking-lot guy said he would pay for the repair, but until then, the door was sealed shut. I could enter my car only from the passenger door.

I completed my tryout that Wednesday and Craig told me to call him on Friday morning. I drove back to Michigan and stopped at the airport to pick up my friend Bob Gordon, who had flown in from New Jersey to join me for a road trip to Florida to attend the wedding of Elisa Freidan. Elisa and I majored in American Studies at the University of South Florida and had become good friends. Our birthdays come two days apart and every year we still call each other in acknowledgement.

Bob and I left Michigan Thursday afternoon in my damaged car. We drove all night down Interstate 75, past Atlanta, until we took a detour for Plains, Georgia, home of President Jimmy Carter.

When we arrived in Plains, on Friday, March 10, I had to find a gas station because I had an important phone call to make. The station I found was owned by Billy Carter, the president's brother, and it was from there that I called John Craig, who offered me a job.

It was agreed my starting date would be March 27. That gave me just enough time to see my mom in Tallahassee, get my car door fixed, attend Elisa's wedding in Jacksonville and drive back to Pittsburgh to find a place to live.

No more picket lines for me. Next stop, Steel City.

*Charley Feeney was the baseball writer for the PIttsburgh Post-Gazette from 1966
until his retirement in 1986*

CHAPTER 12

Charley Feeney

Let me tell you why it was such a treat to watch a baseball game with Charley Feeney, my all-time favorite baseball writer.

Charley started "doing baseball" in 1951 for the New York Star-Journal, and he became good pals with fellow writers Jimmy Breslin and Dave Anderson. As Dave used to say, Charley was "a real newspaper guy."

A native of Queens and a World War II Navy veteran, Charley covered the New York Giants and saw Bobby Thomson's "Shot Heard 'Round the World." In 1966, he came to Pittsburgh to become the Pirates' beat reporter for the Post-Gazette, the paper that hired me as a copy editor in the spring of 1978 after I had spent three cold months on strike in Pontiac, Michigan.

For me, sitting next to Charley was a lesson in baseball dynamics. Always animated, he reminded me of the actor Joe E. Ross (Officer Toody in the 1960s sitcom "Car 54, Where Are You?").

The Post-Gazette newsroom was only a 10-minute walk away from Three Rivers Stadium, so I often spent my lunch hours at the ballpark sitting next to Charley. He would explain to me the ground rules of how to watch a baseball game, what to look for, and he would rant and rave about certain players like Garry Templeton ("the best shortstop in the National League") and Tim Raines ("He can do it all.").

But Charley was never good at remembering first names, so he would call everyone "Pally." At times, he even referred to himself by that name.

Fellow Post-Gazette sportswriter Marino Parascenzo told me about the time Charley called in to the sports desk and said, "Pally, this is Pally. Put Pally on the phone."

Often, Charley would discuss the art of official scoring. I was sitting next to him at a game where Bruce Kison lost a potential no-hitter in the eighth inning on a tricky grounder down the third base line that Phil Garner failed to grab with his backhand. Garner was positioned wide of the bag and even if he had fielded the ball cleanly, in my opinion he had little chance of throwing out the batter, Barry Evans, a reserve infielder the San Diego Padres.

Kison was visibly upset when it was ruled a hit. He gestured angrily toward the press box in the direction of the official scorer that day, Dan Donavan of the Pittsburgh Press.

"Pally, that's not an error," Charley told me. "If the ball is right at you, you expect a major leaguer to make that play. That's why Bill Mazeroski was so good, Pally. He could save your team at least one run a game with his defense."

Two days after the Kison game, both Charley and Dan resigned their posts as official scorers.

One of the most memorable games I ever saw occurred on Saturday, September 30, when the Pirates played the Philadelphia Phillies. I had the best seat in the house — right next to Pally.

For the Pirates, it was their 160th game of the season and with a record of 87-72, the Bucs were 1 1/2 games behind the Phillies in the National League East. If they could win their next two games against the Phils, the Pirates would need to make up a rained-out game in

Cincinnati and a victory there would give Pittsburgh the division crown.

The Pirates had run their winning streak to five by sweeping a twilight doubleheader from the Phils on Friday. Still, only 28,000 fans showed up for Saturday's game. Across town, a crowd of 50,000 watched Pitt play a home football game against North Carolina. No wonder Pittsburgh was considered to be a football town.

Charley jumped out of his seat in the first inning when Willie Stargell hit a grand slam to center field off Randy Learch to give the Pirates a 4-1 lead. But Charley knew this game was far from being over.

"Watch out, Pally, Lerch knows how to swing a bat," he warned me in the second inning.

Sure enough, Lerch blasted a home run to center off Don Robinson and the score was 4-2.

Lerch homered again in the fourth inning, and now it was 4-3. Charley was beside himself after Lerch's second homer, parading in front of the Philadelphia writers, saying, "Did you see that, Pally? What did your Pally tell you? See?"

The Pirates saw their lead vanish when Grant Jackson gave up a three-run homer to Greg Luzinski with two outs in the sixth inning. The score was now 6-4 Phillies and stayed that way until Richie Hebner hit a bases-loaded, bases-clearing double off Kent Tekulve in the eighth inning.

When Hebner scored later that inning on a sacrifice fly, the score was 10-4 and some of the fans headed to the exits. But then came the bottom of the ninth.

Ed Ott, the Pirates' catcher, led off with a single off Tug McGraw. Cito Gaston, the future manager of the Toronto Blue Jays, pinch hit for Jim Bibby and also singled. Frank Taveras beat out a bunt and, as Charley put it, "The bases are drunk with Buccos."

Ott scored to make it 10-5 when Omar Moreno grounded into a force play. Moreno stole second before Dave Parker, on his way to MVP honors, delivered a single to center field to make it 10-7.

Parker took second on the throw home as what was left of the crowd really came alive. Ron Reed relieved McGraw and gave up a single to Bill Robinson. Parker scored and suddenly the score was 10-8 — with the mighty Stargell coming to the plate.

Charley nudged me with his elbow. "Pally, this is it," he chortled. "The season, right here, is on the line."

But Stargell struck out and Phil Garner grounded out and -- just like that -- the game had ended and so had the Pirates' pennant hopes.

I made my way downstairs and into the Phillies' locker room, where there was a celebration in progress. Hebner, who had played the first nine of his 18 major-league seasons with the Pirates, recognized me from having done an interview with him earlier that season and gave me a hug and a hearty handshake.

Garner came over from the Pirates' locker room to shake hands. Danny Ozark, the Phillies manager, poured me a cup of champagne and made a toast with the other writers in the room.

Still, as happy as they were that day, the Phillies didn't get past the Dodgers in the National League Championship Series. As for the Pirates, they beat the Phillies the following day — and one year later they won the World Series.

Charley Feeney retired after the 1986 season and was inducted into the writers' wing of the Baseball Hall of Fame in 1997. Even after I left Pittsburgh in 1983, we stayed in touch. In 1988, after I had started at the New York Post, he saw one of my bylines and sent me a note that began, "Pally, is this you?"

When Charley died at the age of 89 in 2014, I attended his wake on Long Island and thought back to those days in Pittsburgh. How much fun it was watching baseball with Charley and reading his copy.

Yep, Pally -- that was a real treat.

CHAPTER 13

Dan Marino

Dan Marino, to my knowledge, had never smoked a cigar until the day I gave him one in August of 1979.

It was media day for Pitt's football team. Marino was a highly touted freshman quarterback who had opted to stay home in Pittsburgh to play his college football. In fact, his dad was a delivery driver for the Post-Gazette, the paper where I was the editor in charge of producing the football pre-season pullout supplement.

I needed an idea for the cover, and I got one when a city-side reporter named Jim McKinnon came into the newsroom, handing out cigars to announce the birth of his first kid. I took Jim's cigar and headed to Pitt's media day. With a photographer in tow, I walked over to Dan and introduced myself before handing him the cigar.

"Dan, would you mind putting this in your mouth?" I asked.

"Sure," he replied.

We snapped a few photos and I headed back to the office, where I began an extensive library search for another prominent Pittsburgh cigar-smoker. My first thought was Art Rooney, the beloved owner of the Steelers. He always seemed to have a cigar in his mouth.

But then I came across a file photo of Terry Bradshaw with a cigar in his mouth. He and the Steelers were coming off their third Super Bowl title and Pitt was ranked 16th in preseason poll. Hmmm, I thought. This might work.

And, boy, did it ever! I dummied the two images -- Bradshaw on top with Marino underneath — and ran a headline that read, "Pittsburgh's Classy Quarterbacks."

Well, it became a big topic on the Pittsburgh sports radio talk shows. A number of irate fans called in to say it was unfair for the Post-Gazette to put Bradshaw on the cover with an untested freshman quarterback.

Phil Axelrod, our paper's Pitt crack beat reporter, caught some flack when he went to practice the following day. Rick Trocano, not Marino, was Pitt's No. 1 quarterback on its depth charts, having led the Panthers to an 8-4 season in 1978, two years removed from the Tony Dorsett-led team that won the national championship in 1976.

"That kid (Trocano) was in tears," Phil told me later that night. "Everybody on the team felt bad for him."

Well, Trocano now had something to prove. In the opening game, the junior quarterback led the Panthers to a 24-0 victory over Kansas. Marino got to play in the final minutes and his first pass was intercepted. But his third pass that day resulted in a touchdown.

Trocano remained the starter until the seventh game when he injured his hamstring against Navy. Marino came off the bench in the first quarter and led the Panthers to a 24-7 victory, completing 22 of 30 passes for 227 yards and two touchdowns.

From there, there was no turning back. With Marino behind center, Pitt rolled to five straight victories, including impressive wins at West Virginia and at Penn State. That season ended with a 16-10 victory over Arizona in the Fiesta Bowl.

Marino passed for a freshman-record 1,680 yards as Pitt finished 11-1 and was ranked No. 6 in the country. Trocano returned as his backup and eventually was converted to a defensive back for his senior season. He was drafted by the Cleveland Browns and played three seasons in the NFL.

With Marino, Pitt posted two more successive 11-1 records before going 9-3 in 1982, his senior season. He passed for 7,905 yards and 79 touchdowns at Pitt and went on to have a Hall of Fame career with the Miami Dolphins.

Give that man a cigar.

Terry Bradshaw and Dan Marino were featured on the controversial cover of the Pittsburgh Post-Gazette's 1979 football preview section.

CHAPTER 14

Base-brawls

As Rodney Dangerfield might have put it, there is nothing like going to a baseball game and watching a hockey game break out.

Unlike hockey players, though, baseball players are terrible fighters. It's generally a one-swing affair after a brushback pitch and then a bunch of bodies rolling on the ground.

A summer isn't a summer unless one player tries to punch out another, or someone's career is threatened because of a hot-tempered, bench-clearing brawl.

Over the years, a number of brawls have changed or tarnished the careers of several players. Juan Marichal is a good example.

Marichal was a brilliant Hall of Fame pitcher with 243 wins, but he is probably best remembered for an ugly incident that occurred on August 22, 1965, in a game between the San Francisco Giants and Los Angeles Dodgers. While at bat, Marichal clubbed John Roseboro in the head after the Dodger catcher had come close to hitting Marichal while returning the ball to Sandy Koufax.

Players from both dugouts buried Marichal in a near-riot that was broken up by police. Marichal was thrown out of the game, suspended for eight games and fined a record $1,750. He was later sued for $110,000 by Roseboro, who suffered a two-inch gash on the left side of his head.

"There's nothing pleasant at all when you see someone hit in the head with a bat," Koufax said.

Three years later to the date, the career of a young left-hander named Tommy John was jeopardized after a bruising scuffle with Dick McAuliffe at Tiger Stadium. The Detroit infielder charged the mound after a pitch barely missed his head and another was thrown behind him. McAuliffe tackled John and drove his knee into John's pitching shoulder. The shoulder was separated, and John was done for the season.

"I didn't do it purposely, but I know (the White Sox) were trying to take me out of the game," said McAuliffe, who was ejected, suspended for five games and fined $250.

"Dick's a great guy," John told me in 1979. "It just happened. Baseball players, like human beings, are going to get mad. That's why we have murders."

New York teams have seen their share of brawls. The Yankees and Red Sox are no strangers to fighting. In 2003, we saw Pedro Martinez body-slam Yankees coach Don Zimmer. A year later, Jason Varitek stuffed his catcher's mitt up Alex Rodriguez's nose, but that was nothing compared with the 1973 brawl at Yankee Stadium between Carlton Fisk and Thurman Munson.

On August 1, in the ninth inning of a 2-2 game, Munson was racing home after Gene Michael had botched a suicide squeeze. Munson was called out after he barreled into his Boston arch-nemesis, who began punching him with the ball while kicking him. Munson jumped up and he and "The Stick" double-teamed Pudge, who was quickly bloodied.

"It looked like two hookers fighting on 45th Street," said Boston left-hander Bill Lee.

"Ask Fisk who won the fight," was all that Munson said about it.

Fisk was involved in another classic Yankees brawl in 1976 after a hard slide into home by Lou Piniella. When Fisk punched Piniella with the ball, both benches emptied, but the main event shifted to Lee, who was on the mound that night.

Lee, a Yankee killer in the Frank Lary mode, tried to keep Yankee reserve Otto Velez from joining in the brawl and soon found himself under a pile of bodies, where he was stomped upon by Mickey Rivers.

Lee jumped to his feet and started yelling at Graig Nettles, who promptly decked Lee and left him with a damaged left shoulder. The Spaceman was never the same pitcher after that night.

Said Nettles, "I remember what he said a few years earlier about how we fight like Times Square hookers. I just wanted to let him know we had some tough hookers in those days in Times Square."

The Yankees' manager, Billy Martin, was a brawler first class. As a Yankee, he slugged it out with Jimmy Piersall in 1952 and, in 1960 while playing with the Reds, he punched out Cubs pitcher Jim Brewer. When Martin managed the Twins in 1969, he KO'd one of his pitchers, Dave Boswell. In 1979, he decked a marshmallow salesman in a bar brawl.

Martin didn't win them all, however, as he had his lunch handed to him when he took on Ed Whitson in 1985 and suffered a broken arm. The following night, a TV reporter asked Billy why his arm was in a sling.

"I hurt it bowling," he said.

Mets fans will never forget the fight between Pete Rose and Bud Harrelson at Shea Stadium in Game 3 of the 1973 National League Championship Series. Harrelson, the Mets' feisty shortstop, wasn't happy with Rose's hard slide into second base and the two exchanged blows. Both benches emptied and Buzz Capra got into it with the Reds' Pedro Bourbon. Order was restored, but not before the game was nearly called off when fans began throwing objects onto the field.

"It was baseball," Harrelson said. "I had a lot of respect for the way (Rose) played. I just didn't like what he did at that moment."

If you remember when the Giants played at the Polo Grounds, perhaps you can recall the day in 1956 when a pitcher named Ruben

Gomez plunked Milwaukee Braves slugger Joe Adcock on the left shoulder. Adcock was halfway down the first-base line when he charged the mound.

Gomez had the baseball in hand and flung it at Adcock, missing wildly. Gomez then ran from the mound and bee-lined it for the Giants' dugout with Adcock in hot pursuit. Milwaukee's Del Rice was on deck until he raced up the third-base line and dove at Gomez, who evaded the tackle and made it safely into the dugout.

"I had a good chance to get him and I missed," Rice said. "I'll never forgive myself."

Gomez's cowardice left the Giants embarrassed.

"If Gomez had only stayed on the mound," manager Bill Rigney said, "there would have been a brief scuffle and it would have ended with a bunch of bodies on the ground."

In 1953, Gomez nailed Brooklyn's Carl Furillo at Ebbets Field. After reaching first base, Furillo looked into the Giants' dugout and saw manager Leo Durocher taunting him.

Furillo was furious and raced toward the Giants' dugout. One Dodger against a bunch of Giants, Furillo never got close to Leo the Lip during the ensuing scuffle Somebody stepped on Furillo's hand, however, and he was done for the season.

That's basebrawl.

CHAPTER 15

J.R. Richard

There was a time when J.R. Richard was one of the best pitchers in baseball. He never made it to Cooperstown, but I will never forget that one day in 1979 when he treated me like a Hall of Famer.

That spring, I thought it would be a good story for the Pittsburgh Post-Gazette to ask Richard and several other top National League pitchers how best to pitch to Dave Parker, the Pittsburgh Pirates' fearless two-time batting champion. So, while I was down in Florida visiting my mom, I took a ride to a few spring-training sites with this story in mind.

First stop was Vero Beach, where the Dodgers were in camp. First pitcher I approached was Burt Hooton, who was coming off a 19-10 season with a 2.71 earned run average.

Burt, I must say, was not very hospitable. He seemed angry that I would ask him, "How do you pitch to Dave Parker?"

"I'd rather keep that a secret," he barked at me. "I don't want him to know how I pitch to him. He's a very aggressive hitter, so let's just say you pitch him very aggressively. You don't give in to him."

OK ... er, thanks, Burt.

Don Sutton was nearby so I went over and asked him the same question. The future Hall of Famer was a lot friendlier and began to tell me about the time Parker had broken up a potential perfect game in 1976 with a homer.

"I had 22 in a row until I threw a fastball inside," Sutton said. "I believe there is no one way to pitch to him. You try to stay down in the strike zone, and he hits it like a tee shot.

"Parker's the most awesome, devastating hitter in the National League," Sutton said. "He's more selective than (Greg) Luzinski. That means double trouble because there is no way to neutralize (Parker's) power, especially when he's on a binge."

After the Sutton chat, I got into my car and drove 90 miles to Kissimmee, where the Houston Astros trained. When I got there, the Astros were playing, and James Rodney Richard was on the mound.

J.R. was a 6-foot-8 fireballer who led the National League in strike-outs (303) in 1978. I think he was pitching a two-hit shutout that day when he left the game in the seventh inning. Naturally, I wanted to ask him about Parker.

J.R. left the dugout and headed straight to the clubhouse door, where I was there alone, asking him for an interview.

"I can't right now," he said politely. "I'll be glad to talk to you after I finish my workout."

OK, I stayed outside the clubhouse for the next 30 minutes or so, waiting for J.R. Eventually, the game ended, and I was quickly surrounded by a horde of reporters, all eager to talk to him.

When J.R. came out the clubhouse, he looked out at all the reporters and came straight over to me.

"Let's go inside," he told me as he put his massive hand on my shoulder. Turning to the other reporters, he said, "I promised to talk to him first."

I was stunned. He didn't have to single me out like that. After all, I was just another reporter. It made me feel special.

And so I followed him into the clubhouse and asked him, "How do you pitch to Dave Parker?"

"You must be very careful in special situations," he told me. "Parker is a different hitter than anybody else. He will get his hits no matter what you throw. He's a very, very tough out."

When we finished the interview, J.R. shook my hand and wished me well as he went back outside to face the media while I quietly slipped away.

J.R. went on that season to win 18 games and again lead the league with 313 strikeouts and a 2.71 ERA. He, Nolan Ryan and Sandy Koufax are the only modern-day pitchers to strike out more than 300 batters in consecutive seasons.

One year later, at the age of 30, he was 10-4 with a 1.96 ERA at the All-Star break when he began to complain about a dead arm and numbness in his fingers. He missed some starts and went on the disabled list. Some in the media thought he was just being moody and trying to get a new contract. But then came the day J.R. had a major stroke and collapsed on the field during a pre-game warmup.

Doctors found a massive blockage in his right carotid artery and he underwent emergency surgery that evening. J.R. recovered but never again pitched in the majors.

Over the next few years, after his comeback had failed, two divorces and some bad business deals left J.R. a broken man. In 1994, stories began to appear that he was homeless and sleeping under a Houston highway.

Fortunately, he soon turned around his life and began working In Houston with the New Testament Church. He became a minister who continues to work with kids and the homeless.

Nope, J.R. never made it to Cooperstown, but he will always be a Hall of Famer to me.

CHAPTER 16

Letter from Rome

(The following is a letter I wrote to Chris Gargano, my college room-mate, after I took a leave of absence from my job in Pittsburgh and went to Europe, where I took a job in Rome for an English-language newspaper. It was dated May 21, 1982.)

Roomie:

Greetings from Roma! Believe it or not, this is my new home ... well, at least till September 1.

I got a job here working at a newspaper called The Daily American, a paper that is printed here and, I am told, sold across parts of Europe and the Middle East.

The pay ain't great -- I think I can get by on $100 a week. But who cares? I'm in Rome!

Before I get into more details about that, let me tell you about my travels through Europe. It all started with my arrival from Pittsburgh on March 27. I spent four days in London, walking around and drink-ing warm beer at various pubs. I saw some interesting sites such as

Buckingham Palace, Harrad's and the National Gallery and then left town. London was pretty expensive.

On March 31, I crossed the channel and took a train to Paris. What a city! And this marked the first place where I had communication problems other than our dorm parties. French truly is a foreign language to me.

I walked the Left and Right banks so much, my legs got sore. I call it museum-itis. The food was fabulous particularly the French bread and pastries. The women are quite delicious, too. Surprisingly, Paris wasn't as expensive as I thought it would be. My hotel room on the Right Bank near the train station was $15 a night.

The weather was good, except for Amsterdam, where it rained a lot. More on Amsterdam later.

After four days in Paris, it was time to move on and I decided to go to Greece. Originally, I was going from Paris to Spain, but I had my EuRail pass ready to go, so I called an audible and headed south.

Next stop was Geneva, where I spent four days in an expensive but beautiful city. The highlight was the day I took a hike out of town and into the Alps. That morning, near the lake I ran into gentleman from Algeria who was convinced I was an Algerian, too. Even when I showed him my passport, and told him I was a Black American, he didn't believe me. Finally, I gave up and said, "OK, I'm an Algerian."

The next day, I was back on the train heading to Milan, where I met up with two Americanos from Houston. I hung around for one day before catching an afternoon train down the east coast of Italy. Big mistake on Good Friday. The train was packed. I had to stand with "other people" at end of a car. After four hours of that, I got off at Faenza, a small town outside of Bologna. My hotel room that night was $7.50. Nice, too.

The next morning, I wrote you a postcard from a sidewalk cafe. Hope you got it. Back on the train, I made it all the way down to Foggia. That's where I spent Easter morning with the natives.

By that evening, I had reached Brindisi, where I got the 10 p.m. boat to Greece. Boy, was that a long boat ride. We didn't get there till 5 p.m. Monday.

I took the four-hour train ride to Athens and stayed there for four days. I should have stayed two. I saw the Acropolis, and that was about it. I tried to leave that Thursday, but I missed my train because I got lost while stupidly walking to the train station. This meant I had to face another Good Friday exodus because the Greek Orthodox Church celebrated Easter one week later.

In the summer of 1982, Ralph Wimbish worked in Rome as an editor at The Daily American.

Sure enough, the train west to Patras was packed, but fortunately I met a Greek soldier named Chris who befriended me as we stood for two hours at the end of car. Eventually, he went inside and found a seat that we took turns using for the rest of the trip.

Because it was Good Friday, Greek Orthodoxers are allowed to eat only once that day, so at 3 o'clock, everyone seated around me began pulling out food of all sorts. I think they knew I was an American and took pity on me because several of them started passing me things to eat even though I couldn't understand a word they said. I thought it was a really nice thing to do and I tried to thank them the best I could.

I made it back to Italy and hopped on a train to Bari, where I spent the night. The next morning, I boarded a train for Naples, or so I thought. I fell asleep, and the next thing I knew the train was pulling into Rome. I guess I was on the wrong part of the train.

It was about 4 p.m. that, after finding a hotel room, I set off to find the Coliseum. I then picked up a newspaper called The Daily American and went to dinner. I turned to the back page and saw an ad for "experienced journalists."

I went to TDA's office the next day and was hired on the spot. I agreed to work the rest of the week if I was allowed to finish off my EuRail pass. My boss said OK, and on Sunday, April 25, I was back on the train heading to the French Riviera.

I stayed in Monte Carlo for two nights and had a good time. It wasn't as expensive as I thought it would be. My hotel room with a bath was just $15. Without a bath, it would have been $11.

The beach was an amazing thing to see. I forgot that women are allowed to walk around topless. Ouch! I even went for a swim in the Mediterranean, the cleanest blue water I've ever seen. I also went to the big casino and won 10 francs on the slot machines.

After two days, I forced myself to leave Monte Carlo. Next stop was Barcelona, where I split a hotel room with some guy from Kansas that I had met on the train. We drank a bunch of Spanish beer, which is 13 percent alcohol. Three beers here and you're ready to fight bulls.

From Barcelona, I went to Madrid, which might be the cleanest big city I've ever seen. I stayed in a great hotel downtown for $15 a night. Spain is relatively cheap and the food is great. I fell in love with Spanish rice.

I left Madrid on Saturday, May 1, and made it back to Paris by 7:30 Sunday morning. I spent the day walking down the Champs-Elysee and went to see an American movie that wasn't dubbed in French.

The next day, Monday, I headed off to Amsterdam, where I got to meet up with Bill Stieg [my housemate], who had just flown in from Pittsburgh.

Amsterdam kicked ass. The bartender at our hotel called it "sin city." The hotel, by the way, is called "the Hotel California," just like the song. The owner said he likes the Eagles, whom you might remember we saw on September 16, 1972 as an opening act.

Needless to say, I "sinned" in Amsterdam. Heineken, the hometown brew, is sold for 65 cents a glass. And you can buy hashish over the counter. One night, Bill and I wiped out 11 beers and a gram of blond Moroccan without breaking a sweat.

Then there was the "red-light" district. Instead of women standing on corners with their come-ons, they stand or sit in store-front windows inviting you to come in. We went window-shopping. If you see something you like, you knock on the door, she pulls down the blinds and you're in business. It was fun to look, but I did not touch.

The museums and food were tremendous, the best in Europe. For little money, the portions were huge and delicious. I really made a pig of myself, especially with the French fries which come topped with a white sauce that looks like mayonnaise but tastes like vinegar.

I also enjoyed one of best hamburgers ever at a luncheonette near the Anne Frank house. It was a big, round burger filled with cheese and onions on a toasted bun. Wow!

Four nights in Amsterdam, Bill and I parted ways. He headed off to Germany and I went back to Rome, where I started work on May 10. I'm currently staying in a room near the train station for 9,000 lire ($7) a night. For the first few days, I had a hotel room just to the right of the Spanish Steps, but that got too expensive.

Today, I got a call from some guy who is going on vacation for the summer and wants me to caretake his apartment. I'm going to look at it on Sunday. If I get this place and it's conducive for guests, you and Nonie [Chris' wife] got a place in Rome if you'd like to stop by. Rome is quite a beautiful city with no high-rises and a bunch of ruins. I went to the Vatican last week, and it's quite a place.

At work, I'm a news editor and I do the sports page once a week when the sports editor takes his day off. The people at work are nice and I'm teaching some of them the joys of "modular layout." I'm also beginning to pick up some of the lingo.

As for my mother, before I accepted the job here, she had told me she would not be running for a Congress. But then I called her last weekend and she said she is running for a seat in the Florida Legislature. So instead of staying here in Rome until November as I had planned, I'm heading home before September 1 in time for her primary. If she wins, I'm going to Tallahassee and work for her. If she loses, I'll go back to Pittsburgh and start work on November 29. Whatever, we'll see.

In the meantime, I hope everything is OK at your end of the world. Whatever you do, please be sure to write me back. Please! It's a real treat to get mail. I've already received two letters and really enjoyed every sentence.

So, take it easy, stay out of trouble, and I'll see you when I see you.

Ciao,
Wimbish

CHAPTER 17

Bombed in Rome

Somebody set off a bomb at my office building. Somebody could have been killed. That somebody was almost me.

Nobody was hurt after the bomb exploded on May 26, 1982, in Rome, where I was in the second month of working at a English-language newspaper called The Daily American.

A few months before, I was granted a leave of absence from my job in Pittsburgh so that I could help my mother campaign for a seat in Congress. But when the reapportionment wasn't to her liking, she opted not to run, leaving me with eight months to kill. So, I went to Europe and took a job in Rome as news editor at the Daily American.

Having lived in Rome for nearly six weeks, I was somewhat familiar with life and the political intrigue of the Eternal City. Sabotage, kidnappings and even bombings were not uncommon here. But they were typically acts executed at night when there was little or no threat of people being killed.

With President Ronald Reagan coming to town in 12 days, this May 26 bombing was thought to be a warning shot.

I was staying at a pensione near the train station, about a mile away from the office, when I awoke early that sunny Wednesday morning about 6:30. So I decided to come to work well before my 9 a.m. starting time. I took a shower down the hall, grabbed a quick bite at a local breakfast bar and hoofed it to work.

The bomb, police said, went off about 7:45. I arrived about 8 and saw police cars everywhere and didn't know why. I was shocked when somebody told me there was an explosion in my building.

Gregg Szymanski, a co-worker, was in the second-floor newsroom when it happened. He and another staffer opened our office shortly before 7:30.

"I just started my story and I got blown out of my seat," Gregg said later.

Police said the bomb was a timed device packed with a pound of explosives and placed in the lobby of our six-story building on Via Barberini, just down the block from Via Venuto. The explosion blew a hole in the floor but there was no structural damage, so we eventually were allowed inside to go to work.

Our building also housed an American-run, English-language radio station and a group called U.S. Republicans Abroad. Both were headed by Robert Cunningham, an American who also was publisher of our newspaper.

It didn't take long before somebody took responsibility. A phone call to the Italian news agency ANSA claimed a little-known terrorist group calling itself "Communist Groups for the International Proletariat" was responsible for the blast. "This is our salute to American hangman Reagan and all other imperialists," the caller said.

But then, another phone call came in -- not in protest of Reagan's visit, but protesting British intervention in the Falkland Islands. The caller, who said he belonged to the right-wing group Armed Revolutionary Nuclei, said; "This way the English will learn that Italians also know how to explode bombs."

Sorry, wrong country, wrong newspaper. Our 12-person staff consisted mostly of Americans and an Aussie.

Ann Eustice Brandon, the arts page editor from Philadelphia who sat next to me at work, arrived about 9 a.m. She told me it was the first time she had seen, in person, an act of violence.

"This was in your face," she recalls. "The first time I saw violence face to face. I got there and saw the door perpendicular to the floor. This was meant to kill."

As for me, I entered the newsroom that morning amid the confusion. I phoned home as soon as I could to assure my newspaper in Pittsburgh and my mother in Florida that I was alive and well.

Our chief editor, Christopher Winner, assured us we would continue publishing. "We have no enemies," he said, "as far as we know."

Admittedly, I was somewhat shaken and immediately began thinking about taking the next plane home. But as the day went on, I started to think about the beauty of Rome, the food, the gelati, the girls sitting on the Spanish Steps, lunches at the "beeria", and the Pasquino, the English-language movie theater in Trastevere that had a retractable roof.

So, yeah, I decided to stick around. What were the chances of getting bombed again?

And, you know, I'm glad I stayed. I got to celebrate Italy's World Cup victory, ate tons of pasta and scamorza without gaining any weight and met a nice Canadian girl named Janet while forming some other valuable friendships.

Also, I must make note of a weekend trip I took to Yugoslavia during Ferragusto, the festival week in mid-August when most Italians go on vacation.

On Thursday, August 12, I took a train to Trieste and slept in the woods outside of town that night before boarding a train the next morning. I was hoping to reach the seaside town of Dubrovnik by nightfall.

Well, I never made past Zagreb. Every train heading to the Croatian coast that evening was packed beyond capacity.

With time to kill, I had dinner at a nearby restaurant, but I had no idea how to converse with my waiter in Croatian. So, after I pointed to an item on the menu, I was informed by an English-speaking gentle-man at the next table that I had just ordered horse. I recalled the waiter and got a conventional steak — hopefully one from a cow.

After dinner, as evening turned into night, I continued to drink water from a hose at the train station and began to feel woozy with a headache. I think I was getting a case of cholera.

Around 2 a.m., I boarded a train headed for Belgrade, but I jumped off at the last second as it was leaving the station. I instinctively realized something was wrong with me and I knew I had to get back to Italy.

Later, as Saturday morning dawned, I was nearly run over by a truck as I tried to sleep in a nearby parking lot. Fortunately, there was a guy from Madagascar who took note of my sorry state. I never got his name, but he spoke French and did not speak a word of English, yet we somehow communicated. I don't know why or exactly how, but he personally escorted me back to Italy while I slept most of the way. All I remember was that we changed trains in the Slovenian town called Ljubljana.

Later that afternoon, I awoke as the train pulled into the station in Trieste. i immediately looked for my friend to give him my thanks, but he was nowhere in sight. If ever I had a guardian angel, this was him personified.

I made it back to Rome by Sunday night, and two weeks later it was time to head home, back to the good ol' USA. My mother was running for the Florida Legislature and I had to be there to help out.

Ciao, Italia. Hello, Tallahassee.

CHAPTER 18

My Mom

A lawyer, a politician, a trailblazer. Bette Wimbish was all that and more. She was my mother.

My mom died in 2009, but her indomitable spirit is still alive and will be with me till my dying day. Looking back, it still amazes me how well she succeeded with such grace, courage and class in such a hostile environment, in such hostile times. The long, hard road of her life had its share of potholes, twisting turns and untimely detours.

In St. Petersburg, my hometown, she and my dad, Dr. Ralph Wimbish, were right there on the front lines in the fight for civil rights. She was there when my dad slammed Major League Baseball for spring training discrimination. She was there when my dad sued to improve poorly funded Black schools and integrate golf courses. She was there when he led the boycott of department stores and picketed movie theaters, restaurants and the whites-only beaches.

In fact, my mom was always where she needed to be. Often that was our home on 15th Avenue South, preparing family meals daily and driving me and my older sister Barbara and baby brother Terry back and forth to school every day. At nights, when she wasn't reading me bedtime stories, she attended civic meetings, spoke at churches and sometimes found time to play bridge.

When it came to education, she was there pulling me and my sister out of overcrowded Black schools to integrate white ones. Barbara went to high school at St. Paul's; I started sixth grade at St. Joseph's. In 1964, when I became the Jackie Robinson of the Lake Maggiore Little League, she was in the bleachers, cheering me on.

Yes, the times were turbulent. In 1961, I am told a cross was burned in our front yard. Whenever the phone rang, there was always the possibility of a death threat. At the mailbox, occasionally there was hate mail.

And there were some near-tragedies. When I was 3, I nearly drowned in a lake at a picnic in Tampa, but my mom was there to save me. A few years later, when my brother, then 2, fell into the family swimming pool, again she was there.

Otherwise, Bette Wimbish was a fearless political animal who simply never got to fulfill her ambition — to improve the quality of life for the disadvantaged, senior citizens and people of color. If you want to call that socialism, OK, she was a socialist.

In 1960, while pregnant, she ran for the Pinellas County School Board. She lost, but her political career was just getting started. She was determined to get a law degree, so in 1965 she packed up me and my brother and we went to Tallahassee, where she completed law school at Florida A&M, her alma mater, in 2 1/2 years.

Sadly, two weeks before her final exams, my dad died of a heart attack at 45.

Heartbroken but determined as ever, she passed her final exams and began studying for the bar exam just as St. Petersburg became engulfed in a strike by sanitation workers. Naturally, she got involved, and though the strike didn't succeed, it gave her a platform for a run for a seat on City Council in the spring of 1969. Calling for "responsive government" and equal opportunity hiring practices for minorities, she made history, defeating the incumbent, Martin Murray, for the District 6 seat and becoming the first Black-elected official in the Tampa Bay area.

Bette Wimbish began her political career by running for the Pinellas County School Board in 1960. Courtesy Tampa Bay Times

City Council was a real challenge. For the first two years, she grew frustrated by the old guard, four councilmen who blocked just about every initiative she made.

Things got better in 1971 when some of those Council seats changed hands. Her peers elected her vice mayor and she began to get things done, like overhauling the city's water system, improving hiring practices and instituting one of the country's first mandatory seat-belt laws. She also fought unsuccessfully to have Black real estate owners compensated for past discrimination.

In 1972, at the Democratic national convention, she was a Florida at-large delegate who voted for George Wallace. State law mandated she had to vote for the segregationist Alabama governor on the first ballot because he had won the Florida primary. If George McGovern had not received the presidential nomination on the first ballot, she was all in for Hubert Humphrey.

Later that year, she ran for the state Senate and this time she lost. Back on City Council, she felt the urge to return to Tallahassee, primarily because our home had become a prime target of break-ins. One morning, while getting dressed for a City Council meeting, she found an intruder lurking outside our bathroom and banged him over the head with a hand mirror before he ran off.

So, it was no surprise in 1973 when Governor Reuben Askew got her to join the Commerce Department and she moved to Tallahassee. Mom loved Tallahassee. She often talked fondly about her days at FAMU, where she played on the tennis team and was statistician for Jake Gaither's football team.

She soon became deputy secretary of commerce and, later, head of the state's newly formed crime compensation committee.

In 1982, while I was running around Europe, she decided to run for the state Legislature in a Tallahassee district, 250 miles from St. Pete. In a primary field of five, she surprisingly finished first and found herself in a runoff with another Black candidate, Al Lawson.

This was to be her toughest campaign, and I came back from Italy to be her chauffeur. She took a lot of verbal abuse; some of it involving the "C" word. Lawson accused her of being a "carpetbagger from St. Pete" even though she grew up in Perry, Florida, some 45 miles away, and attended high school and college in Tallahassee.

Lawson also said she was "too individualistic" and accused her of being "an elitist." Even worse, he said she was "over educated."

Still, the worst thing said about my mother was that she was trying to pass as white. Yes, my mother was light-skinned, but I can vouch there was nobody prouder of her heritage. Yet, call it a dirty trick or whatever, somebody dug up her voter registration card, which showed her race had been mysterious changed from "B" to "W." That hurt her with Black voters.

She was also smeared in the rural white neighborhoods. From the far reaches of Liberty County, where vote-buying was common, we got wind of a hot rumor that my mom was "secretly married to a Jew." We even got some anonymous phone calls asking if it was true.

Yeah, losing that election was hard for her. Twice, she went to the hospital that fall to be treated for diverticulitis, a painful stomach condition that she may have passed on to me.

Always, though, if you asked her how she was feeling, her standard answer was "fair to middling."

A few years later, Bette's name surfaced as a candidate for the Florida Supreme Court, but she opted to return to St. Pete to run for Congress in 1988. She campaigned on environmental issues, drug education and women's rights. She got 65,000 votes, but that was not enough to unseat Bill Young, the longtime Republican incumbent.

In the early '90s, she was planning on making a run for her old City Council seat just before our family suffered a pair of tragedies. My grandmother Ola Davis, the woman who raised her after my grandfather abandoned them shortly after she was born, died in 1991. Fourteen months later, my brother Terry died at the age of 32.

That really took the steam out of her, and she took a job as local counsel for the Florida Department of Social Services. On the side, she arbitrated labor law cases for the federal government until she retired in 2003.

But there was much more to my mom than just politics. She was a devout Catholic who never swore. I can honestly say I never heard one profane word leave her lips, even on that day I told her I was flunking geometry.

Bette had her quirks. Her great loves included fishing and crabbing, tennis, traveling, making gumbo, Dr. Pepper and Franco Harris, not necessarily in that order. She always was reading books by authors like Tom Clancy and Leon Uris when she wasn't laughing hysterically at TV shows like Green Acres, Taxi and Northern Exposure.

In 2017, the state named a busy highway that leads into downtown St. Pete in her name. Still, my love of sports remains one of her lasting legacies.

Growing up, she took me to baseball games, played catch with me in the driveway and watched football games with me on Sundays.

The only sport she didn't really care for was golf. OK, she wasn't perfect, but was she an exceptional woman? You Bette!

CHAPTER 19

America's Worst Golfer

I was there. I saw it with my own eyes. I saw every single shot when Angelo Spagnolo carded a 66 on the 17th hole at TPC Sawgrass in Ponte Vedra Beach, Florida.

This ugly scene happened in 1985 when Golf Digest conducted a shootout to identify America's Worst Avid Golfer.

The winner -- or loser in this case -- was Angelo, a 31-year-old grocery store manager from just outside of Pittsburgh.

Believe it or not, this so-called tournament was one of golf's biggest stories of the year, and it was my job to promote it. When I started at Golf Digest in 1983 as publicist, I thought I would be working with and writing about the world's best golfers. This tournament, however, I was dealing with the world's worst golfers.

Angelo made it into the tournament's final four which included Joel Mosser, a stockbroker from Aurora, Colorado; Jack Pulford, a restaurant owner from Moline, Illinois; and Kelly Ireland, a lawyer from Tyler, Texas. I can honestly say these guys, or WAGs as we called them, were good guys who loved golf. It was just that they couldn't play a lick.

Angelo Spagnolo, America's Worst Avid Golfer, tees off with Ralph Wimbish in 1985.

"Four men from different parts of the country were bound by a sense of sportsmanship and an abiding love for the game of golf matched only by their inability to play it." — Peter Andrews, Golf Digest

The weird thing is, I might have provided some inspiration for this unsightly contest. In 1984, my game was in such disarray, Golf Digest sent me to one of its golf schools that October. And I must say, thanks to my instructors, namely Bob Toski, Peter Kostis and John Elliott, I did get better. But no way was I ever as bad as these guys.

The criteria to be a WAG finalist was rigid. Basically, you had to be a male, under the age of 55 with no physical handicaps. You had to play at least 21 rounds a year and carry a 36 handicap, then the maximum allowed by the USGA.

Once the word got out that the WAG search was on, Golf Digest quickly received 627 nominations by the spring of 1985. Bob Carney, a senior editor, waded through each nomination and tediously whittled the list down to 12.

Then he personally went out to play a round with each of the "dirty dozen."

Of the 12, Angelo stood out. He was a Pittsburgh guy who had studied journalism at Point Park College, where he had befriended Pete Zapadka, one of my former colleagues at the Post-Gazette. Pete told me that Angelo was a good guy, but he warned me that Angelo was a terrible golfer.

When USA Today did a feature story on Angelo, that's when the WAG story really exploded. Media types from all over the country were calling me to do stories on the selection process. It became a national story when we announced that the final four would play an 18-hole tournament on one of the world's toughest golf courses -- TPC-Sawgrass, the site of The Players Championship. Even Deane Beman, the PGA Tour commissioner, joined the fun and said he would serve as a rules official.

The date for the WAG shootout was set for June 18, a few days after the U.S. Open. My job was to field the dozens of media requests and write press releases about each of the finalists. I also arranged their travel plans to make sure each of them made it safely to Ponte Vedra Beach.

On June 17, the WAGs got to meet each other and play a practice round. Afterwards, Kelly put it best when he said, "I've never seen anything so hard in life. I used every club in my bag (on the par-5 11th hole) and was hitting 24 before I got to the fairway."

Then came the big day. Playing from the back tees, Angelo and Joel were paired in the first group, followed by Jack and Kelly. I told the guys to have their suitcases packed. It was agreed the two guys with the best and worst scores would fly with me to New York that evening to appear on the Today Show early the next morning.

Fourteen camera crews and a slew of writers were on hand at noon when Angelo, dressed in all-white outfit, hit the first shot, right into a water hazard. The gallery was loud and boisterous, including guys wearing T-shirts that read "Angelo's Army" and "I Beat Kelly Ireland Fan Club." Joel was cheered on by members of his regular foursome and Jack's gallery included his mother and his ex-wife, who admitted she wanted to see Jack "make a fool of himself."

The next seven hours were filled with a wide variety of whiffs, chunks and shanks. After nine holes, Joel was the leader with a 75 and a 14-shot lead over Kelly. Jack was in last place with a 104. Angelo was in third place after mis-firing a 99.

Kelly, resplendent in a white Ben Hogan cap and green golf shirt, came charging back and took the lead after making a 12 on the 15th hole. Earlier, Joel had blown an eight-shot lead until he put three balls into the water and took a 25.

The match was still up for grabs when Joel and Angelo arrived at the infamous 17th hole, a treacherous 132-yard par-3 that plays to an island green. Angelo hooked his tee shot into the water and opted to take a drop on a rough patch of grass about 60 yards left of the green. Over the next half hour, he proceeded to splash 26 more wedge shots -- one after the painful other -- into the water.

"Angelo gives a new dimension to the word 'deliberate.' He settles slowly, slowly down in his stance like a nesting chicken, and just as the egg is about to drop he lashes quickly at the ball, sending his woods arching straight into the air while his irons rarely get more than shoulder high." — Peter Andrews, *Golf Digest*

It was an ordeal that was tough to watch. There was no way Angelo, with waist-high shots, was going to hit the ball high enough from that lie to land on that green. Eventually, Angelo begrudgingly decided to use his putter. He took another drop and, now lying 54 on the hole, needed all of 12 putts to get his ball up and through the pathway that leads to the island green and into the hole for his 66. Beman later anointed that pathway "Angelo's Alley."

Asked later how he could possibly score a 66 on one hole, Angelo allegedly replied, "I missed the putt for a 65."

On the par-4 18th, Angelo carded a 22 to seal his place in infamy as America's worst golfer with a score of 99-158--257. That's 185 strokes over par. Minutes later, Kelly sank a 24-foot putt for double-bogey 6 to notch the best score of the day at 75-104--179, 13 shots better than Joel's 75-117--192 and 29 shots better than Jack, who shot identical nines of 104 to finish at 208.

All told, this foursome put 102 balls in the water and took 17 whiffs and 124 penalty strokes. They hit no greens in regulaton, scored no pars and their combined score was 836.

On the 18th green, Angelo was awarded a hideous green-checkered jacket. Everybody applauded. The story, I found out later, made the evening TV news.

Within the hour, Angelo, Kelly and I were rushing to the Jacksonville airport to catch a plane to New York. Believe me, we were dead tired when we got to our hotel, the Carlyle, around 1 a.m., knowing we would be up at 6.

That morning, we took a limo to Rockefeller Center and went straight into the green room for the Today Show. Willard Scott, the weatherman, walked by us, looked at Angelo, smiled and said, "My type of guy." Rita Moreno was there, too, and I, being a West Side Story fan, was honored to sit with her as we watched Angelo and Kelly get interviewed by Bryant Gumbel.

After that, we were back in the limo for a plane ride to Washington for some more interviews with Public Radio and Tony Kornheiser of the Washington Post. At La Guardia, we nearly missed our plane because Kelly had spotted Geraldine Ferraro in front of the terminal and went over to shake her hand.

"I'm Kelly Ireland," he proudly told her. "I'm the best worst golfer in America."

The four WAGs became good friends, went to golf school and appeared at various golf outings over the years to raise thousands of dollars for charity.

Angelo wrote an autobiography called "Life's an ... Unplayable Lie." Joel and Jack went home, retired, but their golf games never got much better. Kelly went back to Texas to practice law. Sadly, he died in 2012.

For years, there was talk about recreating another tournament like this one. But Jerry Tarde, Golf Digest's top editor, nixed the idea when he said: "This extraordinary event will never be duplicated."

Thanks, Jerry, I don't think my eyes could take another one.

CHAPTER 20

George Steinbrenner

George Steinbrenner, as was his wont with the New York City papers, liked making big news splashes, so he prearranged a phone call to the New York Post on July 18, 1990, to tell the world he was "scared to death" of a convicted gambler named Howie Spira.

Major League Baseball was investigating Steinbrenner, the owner of the New York Yankees, for paying Spira $40,000 to dig up dirt on Dave Winfield, one of his star players whom he had just been traded to the California Angels. Steinbrenner and Winfield had been feuding ever since Winfield accused "The Boss" of not making contracted payments to Winfield's charitable foundation.

Steinbrenner had a habit of spreading his "exclusives," making the rounds between The Post, The New York Times, the Daily News, and Newsday. On this day, it was our turn at The Post.

Bob Decker, The Post's sports editor, took me off desk duty to interview Steinbrenner and write the story. I had to go to the office of executive editor Jerry Nachman about 6:30 that evening to take Steinbrenner's phone call. I was joined by Paul Schwartzman, a reporter from the city desk.

Steinbrenner said he became "scared stiff" of Spira after Steinbrenner became aware of a threatening, hand-written letter dated August 25, 1989, that Spira had sent to the FBI.

Spira's letter was obtained by The Post and published on its front page the following day. The letter was addressed to Phil McNiff, a former FBI agent who was head of security for Steinbrenner's ship-building company in Tampa.

In the letter, Spira wrote that his mother was battling cancer and warned McNiff of dire consequences unless Steinbrenner paid him off.

"I swear if anything happens to my mother, George and Dave (Winfield) better both hire a lot of extra security, because then I will really be out of control. I want to come out of this wealthy, or I want to come out of it dead," the letter said.

"I was scared stiff for my family," Steinbrenner told us. "People could say, how could you be scared stiff of a little guy like Spira? But they couldn't protect the pope (John Paul II) and they couldn't protect (Ronald) Reagan.

"If someone is gonna get you, they're gonna get you," Steinbrenner said.

The letter, became part of an eight-count federal indictment charging Spira, who was once employed by Winfield's foundation, with trying to extort Steinbrenner for $110,000.

"I hate George more than even Dave," Spira's letter said.

Steinbrenner told us he was more afraid of Spira than he was of Fay Vincent, the baseball commissioner who had the power to force him to sell the Yankees.

Steinbrenner said he was "fully confident" he would be exonerated by Vincent, who had conducted a two-day hearing that began July 5.

"My lawyers and I feel very good about what has been presented to the commissioner," Steinbrenner said.

Steinbrenner claimed he gave the Spira letter to Vincent in April but didn't discuss it with him at the hearing because Vincent "never asked me about it."

*Backpage exclusive: New York Yankees owner George Steinbrenner told the New York Post why he
feared a convicted gambler named Howie Spira.*

After receiving the letter, Steinbrenner said he immediately increased his personal security.

"We beefed up my security around the clock at my house; hourly visits to my children's houses," he said. "We did all these things and still are (doing them).

"I was scared to death, and I mean it."

Steinbrenner said he considered getting a gun permit but decided instead to hire two around-the-clock bodyguards, both of whom he said were licensed to carry guns.

"We talked to a member of the FBI down there (in Tampa) about arranging a gun permit," he said. "I haven't yet because there is a law in Florida that says you can have one in the glove compartment of your car, but I didn't choose that."

Asked if he had ever been threatened before, Steinbrenner said, "Never like this. I've had my share of fights in my day. My nose is all over the place.

"I had to come forward and make people realize how scared I was for my family," he said. "I've just so much taken a beating from everybody that I really want people to know I was genuinely scared.

"When I say I was scared for my kids and my family, I was scared for my kids and my family," Steinbrenner said. "Down in Tampa, within the last year, a woman went to the police and said her boyfriend threatened to kill her and they didn't pay any attention to her. Damned, if two weeks later, he killed her in a parking lot.

"I'm a big guy. I don't take any bull——, but a little man with a gun in his hand is a big man. I'm scared. If it were your family, you'd certainly be scared, too."

With that, the interview was over. Two weeks later, Steinbrenner wasn't forced to sell the Yankees. Instead, Vincent suspended him from baseball for two years.

The following year, Spira was convicted of extortion and sentenced to two years in prison, a bitter man.

CHAPTER 21

Arlene Howard

When your name is Mrs. Elston Howard, the doors swing wide open and you are treated like royalty on Old-Timers' Day at Yankee Stadium.

Just about every year, Arlene Henley Howard would come to the old ballpark to honor her husband, the great No. 32, the 12-time All-Star catcher, the 1963 American League Most Valuable Player, the man, who in 1955, became the first non-white player to wear the Pinstripes.

Arlene asked me to join her for the 1997 Old-Timers' Game because she wanted me to help her write a book about Elston, which was published in 2001 by Missouri Press. He died in 1980 at the age of 51 after a two-year battle with heart disease.

It was Arlene's idea to have me meet some of her – and Elston's -- favorite people. First, we had to pay homage to The Boss. When you are Arlene Howard, you go first class, which on this day meant tickets to the owner's box. George Steinbrenner was there talking to Joe DiMaggio when we walked in.

"It's always good to have you here," Steinbrenner said as he shot up from his chair to give Arlene a big hug. I got to shake hands with "Mr.

DiMaggio. Steinbrenner, wearing a dark jacket and blue turtleneck, listened intently as Arlene introduced me and told him about the times back in the 1950s, when Elston stayed at my house, in my room, when the spring-training hotels were off limits to Blacks.

Arlene told him about my dad and how he led the fight to end segregation in St. Petersburg before the Yankees got fed up with local politics and moved their spring base to Fort Lauderdale in 1962. The Boss didn't seem to mind that I worked in the sports department at the New York Post, so Arlene and I were allowed to take our seats right in front of Joan Ford, Whitey's wife.

A waiter came down and asked Arlene if she wanted anything. She ordered a hot dog -- with lots of Gulden's mustard.

During the Old-Timer introductions, emcee Frank Messer introduced Arlene. She stood up and waved to the cheering crowd, and it was quite touching to see everyone in the Stadium, including all the old-timers, waving back.

"It's always good to come back," Arlene told me as she fought back the tears. "There were so many good times."

Later, munching on peanuts and Cracker Jacks with DiMaggio sitting across the aisle, Arlene cheered loudly when Chris Chambliss homered. "I knew him when he was, oh, this small," she said recalling the days they grew up in St. Louis.

Graig Nettles, Joe Pepitone, Mickey Rivers, Tom Tresh, Roy White -- Arlene cheered for them all. And Reggie?

"Well, he's mellowed now," she said with a frown. "He had some ego back then."

As David Cone took the mound for the start of the other game that day, it was time to go to the Old-Timers' reception. Steinbrenner stayed behind and gave Arlene a big kiss as she prepared to leave the suite.

The people in the hallways parted as Arlene and Mrs. Ford made their way to the elevator. Lots of smiling faces along the way.

"Pardon me if I have to leave," Arlene said, again fighting back the tears. "Sometimes seeing all these old faces can get pretty emotional."

Arlene Howard is flanked by Bill White, Yogi Berra and Ralph Wimbish at a 2005 exhibit in Westchester County commemorating the 50th anniversary of Elston Howard's rookie season as a New York Yankee.

Suddenly, Diane Munson seemed to come out of nowhere to give Arlene a big hug. She was supposed to be in Steinbrenner's box, but somebody had mistakenly given her seats in left field.

"I had to come to the Stadium on the subway. Can you believe it?" said Thurman's widow, accompanied by Willie Randolph's wife, Gretchen.

Finally, we made it to the Great Moments Room. Hector Lopez was the first player I recognized. When I was a kid in St. Pete, Lopez and Elston were frequent visitors to the Wimbish house during spring training. Hector didn't remember me, but it pleased me that he had fond memories of my dad.

"Hey, Maestro," shouted Horace Clarke as he greeted Lopez. Cliff Johnson stepped forward, looking just as intimidating as he did when he once rumbled with Goose Gossage in 1979.

"Elston never would have allowed that fight to happen," Arlene said about the shower wrestling match that KO'd Gossage and the Yankee pennant hopes that season.

Arlene took a seat and began to hold court.

"Hello, Arlene, I'm Stan Bahnsen," said a familiar face. The 1968 AL Rookie of the Year said Elston "... was my first catcher when I came up in 1966. He was one great guy."

Phil Linz came over and offered more praise. "You know, Elston was the best catcher the Yankees ever had. Munson was good, but he wasn't in Elston's league. Nobody had an arm like Elston."

When Jim Bouton of Ball Four fame walked past, there was no exchange of pleasantries. "I want nothing to do with him," Arlene told me. "What he said in that book (about Elston) was unforgivable."

Ron Guidry was sitting with Dick Tidrow and Sparky Lyle until he spotted Arlene. "He was one of Elston's favorites," Arlene said. "He was always so polite with his 'yes, ma'am' and 'no ma'am.' He'd always invite everybody over for those big parties. He's Cajun, you know. Oh, what food!"

The Yankee fan inside of me wanted to tell Guidry about the night of June 17, 1978, when I sat upstairs in Section 3 and saw him strike out 18 California Angels. I still have the scorecard I kept that night.

Arlene asked Guidry if Reggie was around.

"No, ma'am," said Guidry, who proceeded to tell Arlene about the time her husband slam-dunked Jackson into a garbage can in 1977.

"We were celebrating having won the pennant, drinking champagne, and Reggie was shaking up the bottles, spraying everyone," Guidry recalled.

"Ellie came over and told him that he had an eye problem and didn't want any champagne in his eyes. Reggie kept spraying, and Ellie came over with those huge hands he had, picked Reggie up and slammed him head-first into a garbage can. I'll never forget it."

Whitey Ford, the Chairman of the Board, came over to the table and made my day when he told me he remembered my dad and what he did to help out Elston in the early '60s.

"Whitey was always very close with Elston," said Arlene, recalling the time their two families did an oatmeal commercial. "Whitey and Yogi. It's a shame that Yogi is not here."

Steinbrenner and Berra had been feuding since 1985 when Steinbrenner fired Berra as Yankee manager. Berra stopped coming to Old-Timers' games because of it and the feud lasted two more years until they buried the hatchet in 1999.

The feeling among some of the more veteran Yankee players and officials is that Elston would have never let the feud last that long.

Yes, Elston Howard could have done that, too.

CHAPTER 22

Hank Bauer

In 1955, when the time finally had come to integrate the Yankees, Hank Bauer came through in the clutch – much the same way as he had done so many times during his 14-year major-league career.

On a team where the manager called Elston Howard "8-Ball" and occasionally let the N-word fly, Bauer did his part in making sure the First Black Yankee felt comfortable in pinstripes.

"He was very personable; such a good friend to Elston," Arlene Howard recalled when informed of Bauer's death in 2007.

"He was tough-looking, but he was honest and fair. Back then, when America was such a racist country, I don't think race ever crossed his mind. He thought of you as a person."

Yep, this tough-looking ex-Marine with the crewcut was a valuable friend and ally to Elston – in and out of the Yankee clubhouse. Bauer and Howard had a lot in common -- both grew up in the St. Louis area; both served in the armed forces before they wore pinstripes; and both were "victims" of Casey Stengel's platoon system.

Together, as teammates, they helped the Yankees win four straight American League pennants (1955-58), including World Series titles in '56 and '58.

Hank was notorious for barking at Yankees rookies. "Don't mess with my money," was one of his favorite sayings. But as soon as he saw the way Elston hustled in the spring of '55, he knew that wouldn't be a problem with Howard.

Yankee mystique? Hank admittedly was a big believer. He lockered right next to Elston and gave him tips on playing the outfield, when to take batting practice, what to look for in certain pitchers and, of course, how to "act like a Yankee."

In fact, whenever somebody in the stands would yell racial slurs at Elston, it was Hank who was the first to stick his head out of the dugout to stare down the loudmouth. When a reporter asked why he would do such a thing, Hank replied, "because he is my friend."

Before the '55 season opened, the Yankees played an exhibition game in New Orleans, where "colored" were allowed to sit only in the left field bleachers. Stengel's lineup that day included Elston in right field and Bauer in left field.

"First inning, you wouldn't believe what [the white fans] called me," Elston said. "So, Bauer suggested we be switched. And so, the next inning, Stengel put me in left field with my people."

Later that season, when the Yankees were in Chicago, a group of Yankees were eating breakfast at a big round table at the Del Prado Hotel, where they were staying.

"Elston came in the room and there was an empty seat right next to me," Hank recalled. "He saw the seat and hedged a bit. I motioned for him to come sit with us. When he sat down, I told him, 'You play with us, you eat with us. You're one of us.'"

Arlene recalled how sad Elston was when Hank was traded to Kansas City after the 1959 season. The Yankees got Roger Maris in that deal, but Elston felt like he had lost a good friend.

"Elston always thought the world of him because of his hustle," Arlene said. "He wasn't born a great player, but it was his hustle that made him great."

After leaving the Yankees, Hank managed the A's for two seasons before joining the Baltimore Orioles as their first base coach. In 1963, he was named manager and piloted the O's to the World Series title in 1966. In 1968, he was fired and replaced by Earl Weaver.

Bauer eventually retired to the Kansas City area and died on February 9, 2007 at the age of 84, a victim of lung cancer.

CHAPTER 23

George Crowe

It wasn't often the original "Big Daddy" would come down from the mountains to talk baseball, the game he once loved. George Crowe was reclusive and generally preferred to stay home in his cabin deep in the Catskills, where he would hunt and fish.

Crowe never paid much attention to modern-day baseball, either -- except when it was World Series time.

"I've always been pretty much of a loner," Crowe, an avid outdoorsman, told me in 1997 when I was researching the Elston Howard book.

"Hunting is my game now," he said, sitting back in a chair in the kitchen of Arlene Howard. They became good friends in the 1950s when George and Elston played winter ball in Puerto Rico. In fact, George can be seen in the Howard family home movies, taking a dip with Elston in the Wimbish swimming pool.

George also was quite a basketball player. In 1939, he was Indiana's first "Mr. Basketball" and, after a World War II stint in the Army, he played pro basketball for the Los Angeles Red Devils in the late 1940s. One of his teammates was Jackie Robinson.

As a ballplayer, George barnstormed the country with Roy Campanella's All-Stars. But just like Ernie Banks, he never played in the World Series.

"That's what everybody wants to do; get to the World Series," George said. "I just didn't get there."

Long before there was a Cecil Fielder, George was a 6-foot-2, 210-pound left-handed slugger who played first base in the Negro leagues. He played in the old Yankee Stadium for the Black Yankees before the team went belly up after the 1948 season.

After a stint with the Newark Eagles, he was signed by the Boston Braves in 1949. Called up in 1952 at the age of 31, he spent 10 seasons with the Braves, Reds and Cardinals.

Back then, George, who was born in 1921, was the "Big Daddy" of Black ballplayers. The nickname, which he never cared for, was given to him by a bunch of St. Louis writers late in his career and was perpetuated by younger teammates Bob Gibson and Curt Flood.

"George was an early leader in encouraging and helping young Black players on how to survive the early restriction and insults, both on and off the field," said Bill White. "He helped Flood and many of us players when he joined the Cardinals and was our spokesman with the front office. George was someone all the players, Black and white, respected."

George told me he believed his best chance at getting to the World Series came in 1956 when he played for Cincinnati. The Reds finished two games behind the Brooklyn Dodgers that season with Birdie Tibbetts as manager.

"We had a manager who didn't want to win the pennant," George said. "We had a pitcher named Brooks Lawrence who won 13 straight games. But Birdie Tibbetts came out one day and told someone, 'Ain't no Black man's going to win 20 games for me.' And he refused to pitch Lawrence after he got 19 wins."

Nope, George hadn't forgotten the days when Black ballplayers were treated as second-class citizens. He never forgot when he had to sleep in different hotels and eat in different restaurants.

George Crowe, before he played baseball in the major leagues, was Indiana's first "Mr. Basketball" in 1939. Courtesy Indiana Basketball Hall of Fame.

"It didn't really bother me that much 'cause I knew that was the way it was," he said. "You knew what you were getting into."

Asked to name his two least favorite cities, George took a deep breath before he said, "Cincy and Philly were the worst, I'd say. Back in the '50s, they all were bad."

"Chicago fans were rough on me," he said. "One time, after I hit a pinch-hit home run off Warren Hacker to break up a no-hitter in the ninth inning, I thought they wanted to lynch me."

George's biggest gripe was that he spent too much time on the bench. In 1956, he hit 10 homers as backup to Ted Kluszewski. Crowe's best season came in 1957 when he hit 31 homers, most of his ABs coming about after Kluszewski got hurt.

That season, a ballot-stuffing campaign saw seven of George's Cincy teammates voted into the National League's starting lineup. George was beaten out by Stan Musial.

In 1958, George was named to the National League All-Star team, but did not play in the game.

That summer, he also had the rare distinction of being a left-handed second baseman. For two-thirds of an inning, George switched positions with Johnny Temple and helped turn a double play.

Chicago Cubs manager Bob Scheffing was not impressed. He played the game under protest because George had used an oversized first baseman's mitt. The protest led to a rule change that mandated first basemen must use a standard glove when changing positions.

Soon after, Crowe injured his knee at Forbes Field in Pittsburgh.

"I was never the same after that," he said.

In 1959, George was traded to the Cardinals, only to find Musial playing first base. Coming off the bench, he led the National League in pinch-hits with 17.

Two seasons later, in 1961, George Crowe retired. In 702 games, he had a .270 batting average, 81 home runs, 299 RBIs and a whole lot of memories.

He died in January of 2011, two months before his 90th birthday.

CHAPTER 24

Buck O'Neil

There always was a sparkle in Buck O'Neil's eyes when he talked baseball. Years after his passing, the game could surely use that sparkle.

From Babe Ruth to Satchel Paige, Jackie Robinson and even Alex Rodriguez, Ol' Buck saw them all, uh-huh. The legendary Kansas City Monarchs player-manager and Ken Burns TV documentary star, who died on Oct. 6, 2006 at the age of 94, knew just what role they all played in the history of his beloved game.

"I know why A-Rod's coming to New York," Buck told me in 2004 after Rodriguez was traded to the Yankees.

"He could have gone to Boston, played in Fenway Park. See? But he had a chance to play in Yankee Stadium. Play there every day. That's top of the line.

"Mmm-hmm, like Count Basie, you've got to come to New York City, the cream. Uh-huh, you come to the Apple."

Mmm-hmm. Even then, Buck said he believed A-Rod playing in New York was good for the game, like Bo Jackson was when he played for the Kansas City Royals in the late 1980s.

"He might have been the best athlete in the world," Buck said, referring to Jackson.

"I heard Babe Ruth hit the ball, and the bat had a different sound to it. I heard that sound again, uh-huh, when I saw Josh Gibson. The next time I heard that sound, it was Bo Jackson."

Buck said he didn't like all the noise he was hearing about steroid use.

"Black players are being painted into a corner," he said. "If you aren't white and hit 70 home runs, somebody's going to accuse you of something.

"As long as you're in this country, it's Black and white, you see. You know about that (2004) Super Bowl? They didn't say anything about the man (Justin Timberlake) who pulled off that girl's (Janet Jackson) top."

This was not the first time I had met Buck. In early 1999, Arlene Howard and I flew to Kansas City, where Elston had started his professional career in the Negro leagues with the Monarchs. We wanted to talk to Buck, who was Elston's manager. That evening, Buck, then 87 years old, drove us to dinner at this favorite rib joint, Gates Bar-B-Q.

Buck once was a member of the Baseball Hall of Fame's "veterans committee." Because of him, a good number of Negro league stars – Josh Gibson, Judy Johnson, Oscar Charleston, Willie Wells, to name a few -- have plaques in Cooperstown.

That veterans committee was abolished after 2001, and in 2016, an "early baseball" committee was formed to meet every 10 years to vote for forgotten Negro league legends. That committee is scheduled to meet again in December 2021.

Buck himself was nominated on a special Hall of Fame ballot for Negro leaguers in 2006 but amazingly came one vote shy of getting in.

"God's been good to me," Buck said after the announcement. "They didn't think Buck was good enough to be in the Hall of Fame. That's the way they thought about it, and that's the way it is, so we're going to live with that.

"Now, if I'm a Hall of Famer for you, that's all right with me."

Buck O'Neil, the legendary player-manager of the Kansas City Monarchs, for many years was the voice of the Negro Leagues. Courtesy Negro Leagues Baseball Museum.

Bob Kendrick, president of the Negro Leagues Baseball Museum in Kansas City, told me he believes this time around Buck should make it to Cooperstown.

"He checks all the boxes," Kendrick said. "He was an outstanding player, a good hitter and a stellar first baseman. He broke barriers being the first Black coach (with the Chicago Cubs in 1962) in the major leagues. And he became the voice of the Negro leagues, no doubt he belongs in the Hall of Fame.

"They want him in there."

Buck told me he wanted to see Gil Hodges, Bill White and Elston Howard get into the Hall, but he was against Pete Rose.

"Even if the commissioner makes him eligible, he won't get in," Buck said of Rose, baseball's all-time hits leader. "He committed a cardinal sin. He gambled on baseball."

To his dying day, Buck toured the country promoting the game, particularly the Negro League Baseball Museum, which he was instrumental in its founding in 1990. He also was a big supporter of educational programs like Harlem RBI, which encourages inner-city kids to play baseball.

"It's doing what it's intended to do," Buck said. "Create and generate interest in baseball. It's good for the game."

Uh-huh. That's what Buck liked to see with those sparkling eyes.

CHAPTER 25

Bill White

Bill White was vacationing in Canada when he got the sad news in 2007 about Phil Rizzuto.

"Well, I had seen Phil 10 days ago," White told me from his summer home in Gananoque, Ontario. "Let's just say Phil's in a better place now. He was a good man, a good guy. He's in a better place."

For 18 years White shared the Yankees' broadcast booth with Rizzuto, who died August 13, 2007 at the age of 90 from complications due to pneumonia.

Bill was the first African American to do play-by-play regularly for a major-league team, and he was a member of baseball's old "veterans committee" that voted The Scooter into the Hall of Fame in 1994. Yogi Berra, Ted Williams, Pee Wee Reese, Buck O'Neil, Pittsburgh Pirates general manager Joe L. Brown and St. Louis sportswriter Bob Broeg were also members of that committee, which was disbanded and revised in 2001 after they voted Bill Mazeroski into the Hall.

"Phil was unique, a great broadcaster who was extremely popular," Bill said. "If he hadn't made it into the Hall of Fame as a player, he would have made it as a broadcaster.

"Nobody wanted ballplayers in the broadcast booth when he got hired. That's one reason he made it so easy for me."

Before White accepted the Yankees job in 1971, he phoned Larry Doby, the Cleveland Hall of Famer who in 1947 became the first African American to play in the American League.

"I called him and Elston Howard to ask about Phil," Bill said. "Larry told me about how Phil went out of his way to make him feel welcome even though he played for another team. Some of his own teammates wouldn't shake Larry's hand, but Phil encouraged Larry, and he did the same with Elston.

"I came [to New York] with a good feeling, and Phil made me feel welcome. He helped me in my broadcasting."

When Bill made his debut in the spring of 1971, he was introduced on the air by Whitey Ford. Ironically, the first words spoken by a minority sportscaster were "Thank you, Whitey."

Bill is fondly remembered by Yankees fans for the way he often would play straight man for Rizzuto's broadcast-booth antics.

"When I took the job, the Yankees weren't playing well," Bill recalled. "We had to get a schtick to keep things entertaining, and it just carried over when the Yankees got good around the time they signed Reggie Jackson. When they had those good teams, with Lou Piniella and Thurman Munson, we had to do baseball."

Bill left the Yankees' broadcast booth in 1989 to become National League president. My first backpage for the New York Post came on the day he accepted that job. My headline read, "MR. PRESIDENT."

Bill said his most memorable moment on the air was the time in Milwaukee when The Scooter introduced himself at the start of the broadcast as "Bill White."

Also, there was the time in Boston just moments after Bill had called Bucky Dent's home run ("Deep to left...") in the 1978 playoff game against the Red Sox.

"Don't ask me to say anything, I've been holding my breath, Bill White," Rizzuto said.

"What did you think about that ball up there on the screen?" Bill asked.

"I was in the press room with all those Red Sox fans, and when Bucky hit it, I let out three 'Holy Cows!' and I thought Frank Malzone (former Red Sox third baseman) was gonna bite me on the ankle."

"There were so many things we had fun with," White said. "The rapport was genuine."

Rizzuto is a Hall of Famer, but White is still awaiting his call. His credentials are impeccable, and his career was historic.

As a player, White was the first to speak out against spring training segregation in 1961.

"What happened is that Dr. Ralph Wimbish of the NAACP had a friend who was a dentist (Robert Swain) who wanted to dock his boat at the St. Petersburg Yacht Club, and they wouldn't let him do it. That upset me a bit," Bill recalled in his 2011 autobiography *Uppity: My Untold Story About The Games People Play.*

"Then one day when I went into the clubhouse, I saw the list of people who were asked to go to the community breakfast and I said, 'Wait a minute.' These business guys are leasing public property and they won't allow a minority to deck his boat there. They don't want minorities. That's what started it."

A sure-handed first baseman, Bill won seven Gold Gloves and still holds the record for most unassisted double plays in a season at first base (8 in 1961). He was an eight-time All-Star and won a World Series ring with the Cardinals in 1964, the year he finished third in MVP balloting.

Bill made his major league debut with the New York Giants on May 7, 1956 and homered off Ben Flowers in his first at-bat.

"St. Louis had that short right-field fence," Bill recalled. "It was just 322 to right-center field. I hit a line drive that just went over. I wasn't elated. It's just what I was supposed to do."

A stint in the Army forced Bill to miss all of the 1957 season and most of 1958. On April 12, 1960, he singled off San Francisco Giants starter Sam Jones – the man the Cardinals traded for him in 1959 – to record the first base hit at Candlestick Park.

One of his best games came in May 30, 1960 at the Los Angeles Coliseum when he homered twice off Don Drysdale and had a career-high 6 RBIs.

"He threw spitballs," Bill said of Drysdale. "It actually was oil he kept on the back of his hair. And when you loaded the ball up, it sunk. I was a low-ball hitter. He was throwing to my strength."

Bill, who had seven career homers off Drysdale, finished his playing career in 1969 with a .286 career batting average, 202 homers, 870 RBIs and 103 stolen bases.

As a broadcaster, in 1971 he broke the color barrier when the Yankees put him in their broadcast booth. He also did games for CBS Radio and nationally televised games for ABC.

Marty Appel, Yankees historian and former Yankees public relations director, told me there's good reason why Bill is still revered by fans who watched televised Yankee games between 1971 and 1988.

"He brought a deep knowledge of the game, a great insight of players, and a clever sense of humor to the booth," says Marty, author of *Pinstripe Empire: The New York Yankees From Before Babe To After The Boss*. "He turned out to be a wonderful foil for Phil Rizzuto and a great compliment to Frank Messer. He worked hard at his new craft. It was a perfect fit and Yankee fans embraced him from day one, despite his lack of Yankee -- or in fact, American League DNA."

As National League president, he oversaw the placement of expansion teams in Denver and Miami and prevented a move that would have seen the San Francisco Giants relocate to St. Petersburg in the early '90s.

"He basically said, 'Over my dead body,'" says author Peter Golenbock. "He arranged for a different group, one from San Francisco, to buy the team and keep it in the Bay Area.

"He is one of the greatest human beings I have ever known," Golenbock says. "He was treated shabbily by the Jim Crow racists in St. Petersburg when he played for St. Louis."

A modest man of great integrity, Bill has since turned his back on baseball and enjoys retirement. In 2021, he turned 87 years old. Before the Covid-19 pandemic, he spent his time traveling, seeing his family and fishing. But he doesn't expect to see his plaque in Cooperstown.

"That's not for me," Bill told me in 2019. "The whole process is too political. I want no part of it."

No matter. It's a shame Bill White is not in the Hall of Fame. He belongs.

Ralph Wimbish's first back page for the New York Post.

CHAPTER 26

Doc Rot

Once upon a time, deep in the urban jungle of New York sports journalism, there was a man who emerged from virtual obscurity to specialize in the diagnosis and treatment for the pandemic that became fantasy baseball. His name was -- well, let's just call him Dr. Rotisserie.

The good doctor, known as Doc Rot to friends and colleagues alike, was a baseball brainiac who was the Sanjay Gupta of his time. Starting in 1989, the New York Post published a weekly column in which Doc Rot would advise lovelorn rotisserie baseball owners on how to deal with their ailing teams.

Unlike his cohorts Hondo and Mr. Loser, Doc Rot was a humble man. He was easily identified by the surgical mask he always wore in public with his baseball cap slightly askew. Some thought he was homeless because he occasionally was spotted outside the South Street Diner muttering Don Mattingly's name to anybody passing by.

Doc Rot usually would get two or three letters a week seeking advice. It is assumed his readers followed his sage advice. Often, when he needed column material, he would call up Meat Market Mike, the pseudonym of a semi-crazed rotisserie owner who went by the name of Michael Curry.

Doc Rot's co-workers were so enamored with his various talents, the office golf tournament was renamed The Doc Rot Open in his honor and played annually at some of the top golf courses in the New York metropolitan area.

In 1994, however, Doc Rot disappeared under mysterious circumstances. One rumor was he jumped off the Brooklyn Bridge because he had predicted a Hall of Fame career for Mel Hall. Another rumor was that he had burned out and left the rotisserie business entirely and moved to North Carolina to play golf.

Recently, an old VCR tape surfaced from 1992 in which Doc Rot made a rare appearance on The Joe Franklin Show. We now join the program already in progress.

Joe: Hello, my friend. What a surprise, I must say. It's good to finally meet you.

Doc: Well, thanks, Joe. I always try to watch your show, just before the 2:30 highlights on ESPN.

Joe: Thanks, Doc. Hey, you know what? I was eating a wonderful Reuben, a really good one, the other day at the Second Avenue Deli, when Murray, that great old singing waiter who played Riff in the 1962 off-Broadway production of West Side Story, told me about your new book.

Doc (Extinguishing his cigarette): Ah, sorry, Joe. I haven't had time to write one. I just came here tonight to advise your viewers about the importance of starting pitchers this time of year.

Joe: OK, OK. Ah, it says here, my stage director informs me, rotisserie GMs will be making a slew of trades before the August 1 trading deadline. What can you tell us?

Doc: Joe, I think you gotta look at some of these starting pitchers with high ERAs or losing records and try to swing a deal or two.

Joe: Is that so? By the way, Gina Bastow, that talented young soprano who's knocking them dead over at the Rainbow Room, will be coming right out after a word ...

Doc (interrupting): Joe, suppose you have Mark Langston on your team. What do you do with a 4-13 pitcher who has lost eight straight games?

Joe: Doc, I thought Langston was that very funny comedian who was opening for Harvey Mertz next week through Thursday up at Kutsher's.

Doc: Everyone knows Langston is a joke this time of year. Every draft auction makes him out as a guy who can bring you plenty of strikeouts. But look at his ERA and ratio, particularly this year.

Joe: A bum, right? Like the ones who played in Flatbush?

Doc: You said it, Joe. But one of the funny things about running a rotisserie team is that you gotta take chances. I say right now is the time to pull off a Langston-type deal if you can.

Joe: Yes, I see. But what if your team is out of it, like the time Jiggy Malone fell off the stage over at Roseland?

Doc (coughing): Teams rebuilding for next year should always be on the lookout for underachievers who are having off seasons. Like Henny Youngman might say, take Joe Magrane, Chris Bosio, Jim Deshaies and Greg Ballard — please.

Joe: Well, unfortunately, Mr. Rotisserie, my friend, it looks like we're headed for a station break. Perhaps you can hang around, maybe have a Hoffmann's Ginger Ale?

Doc: Sorry, Joe, I gotta go. It's Friday night, coming up on 2 a.m., and I gotta get out to my car and listen to Jody McDonald read all the box scores on WFAN.

Joe: Well, then. We'll be right back with the Nordy Grissom Trio, and later on, the Cunningham Brothers. Don't touch that dial.

CHAPTER 27

Tiger Woods

The "second best golf shot" I ever hit was so good, Tiger Woods came over to me and shook my hand. That memorable shot happened on a cloudy day in early June of 1994 at Saint Andrews Golf Club in Hastings, New York.

Tiger, an 18-year-old amateur at the time, had just arrived that morning with his dad Earl from California. Tiger had received a sponsor's exemption to play in that week's Westchester Classic, and he was at Saint Andrews to do a junior golf clinic sponsored by NYNEX and the Met PGA.

When I arrived at Saint Andrews that morning, Tiger was on the far end of the driving range hitting golf balls while Earl was holding court with the media. It was hard focusing on what Earl was saying while his son was blasting out shot after shot with the greatest of ease.

The clinic began with about 12 select juniors sitting attentively in chairs. Earl took the microphone while Tiger, wearing a Cleveland Indians baseball cap and chewing hard on his gum, continued to hit balls. Jim Thorpe, one of the PGA Tour's top players back then, was there, too.

"Tiger started when he was six months old," Earl told the kids. "I wanted to do that because I made the mistake of not taking up the game when I was a young man. He's been playing competitive golf since he was 4 years old. His mother would drive him to play in nine-hole tournaments."

Earl continued to talk about Tiger's development into a top-ranked junior at age 13. Somebody asked Earl if he had set any goals for his son.

"I don't set goals for him," Earl said. "I learned a long time ago he has the ability to set his own goals. His goals are much more stringent than any I would arbitrarily set for him. But I do see him as a success on the tour, because, frankly, he has it all."

When Tiger came to the microphone, he was asked about his decision to attend Stanford University that fall instead of turning pro.

"It was a very easy decision," he said. "Going pro never entered my mind. There's too much experience to be had in college. It's going to be a lot of fun. I've got a lot of growing up to do, mentally and physically."

Tiger was asked if he had any long-term goals.

"I don't tell anyone my goals except my father. They're very personal," he said. "I'm going to get through college in four years; it's going to be rough. I'll apply myself 100 percent and after I get through that, I'll turn pro."

Tiger then talked about his dad.

"My father always said that you learn from your failures. We can talk about anything, anytime. Talk about school, relationships, drugs, anything. I'm very fortunate to have a relationship like that," he said.

Tiger was asked if he was the great "Black Hope."

"To be honest, I really don't like that 'Black Hope' stuff," he said. "I'm mostly Asian anyway. My mom's Thai and I got some Chinese from my father's side. Add it all up I'm over 50 percent Asian and a little bit Black. But in this country, I'm categorized being Black because I have a Black father.

"Golf originated as a white, upper-class sport and it's time this changed because society is changing. It's becoming more mixed, so let's integrate this thing."

Eighteen-year-old Tiger Woods was all smiles at junior golf clinic held in 1994 at Saint Andrew's Golf Club in Hastings, New York. Courtesy Bruce Smith / Sporty Bear Productions

When the clinic ended and the golf outing started, Tiger jumped into a cart and drove around the course, playing a hole or two with each group. Each foursome included a media member and at least one of the junior golfers from the clinic.

"It was really fun watching Tiger drive his cart around like a crazy teenager," recalled Jean Schob, who was then the Met PGA's director of junior golf and ran the clinic.

"I was engaged at the time and my future husband was there and I kept calling him 'honey.' Tiger picked up on that and for the rest of the day all I heard was 'Hun-nee, Hun-nee.'

"Looking back, it was so nice to see how human he was compared to the professional he is now. He was just a kid having fun."

Tiger played the 383-yard fourth hole with veteran sportswriter Chuck Stogel and his group.

"Tiger impressively crushed a 3-wood over the left corner of the dogleg that landed beyond the creek and maybe 60-70 yards from the green," Chuck recalled. "He wedged it up to eight feet and sank the putt for birdie.

"Meanwhile, I hit a balloon tee shot that didn't reach the dogleg. I hit an iron over the creek, short of the green, chipped on and two-putted for a bogey."

As for my foursome, Tiger caught up with us at the 15th hole, a 350-yard dogleg right, with a big pond fronting the green. I had smacked my drive about 225 down the middle before Tiger's cart pulled up beside my ball. He shook hands with everyone in my group before he threw down a ball next to mine.

From about 125 yards out, I stepped up to my ball, took a deep breath and launched a beautiful 9-iron over the water, straight at the flag. The ball just missed the cup and settled about three feet away.

Then it was Tiger's turn. He took out what looked to be a wedge and hit a good shot that finished, I'd say, about 10 feet from the cup.

Tiger had a smile on his face when he came over to me, shook my hand again and said, "It was nice to meet you, sir."

With that, Tiger jumped back into his cart and sped away into golf history.

A few days later, he shot rounds of 75 and 70 and missed the cut at the Westchester Classic by one shot. Later that summer, he won the first of his three straight U.S. Amateur titles. He spent two years at Stanford before turning pro in 1996.

As for me, I continued to dwell in golf mediocrity for the next 11 months until I hit my "best shot ever" -- a hole-in-one. And won a new car.

CHAPTER 28

Hole-in-one

Every golfer dreams about getting a hole-in-one. When my "dream" came true, a new car came along with it.

I hit the golf lottery on May 15, 1995, in a charity outing for Juvenile Diabetes at Quaker Ridge Golf Club in Scarsdale, New York.

It rained that morning and I almost decided not to go. In the end, I just couldn't pass up playing Quaker Ridge, one of the top-ranked golf courses in the country. Very private. Very exclusive. Beautiful course.

Playing in a fivesome with two caddies, the round started slowly. I was doing OK until I missed a three-foot par putt on the par-4 eighth hole. Incensed, I stomped over to the tee box of the 157-yard ninth hole.

I was so ticked I didn't realize it was the "car hole" as I pulled out my trusty Ping Eye2 6-iron. I hit my shot, a low liner that hit the front of the green and began rolling toward the flagstick in the back corner of the green.

The ball went over the hill and disappeared.

Somebody yelled out, "It's in the hole!"

Without hesitation, I ran to the green to see if my ball was in the cup. It was. It was my second ace, the first coming at Yale's golf course in 1990.

I took my magic ball, a Titleist DT with a red 1 on it, out of the cup and turned to see my playing partners -- John Groesbeck, John Tracy, Vincent Sweeney and Paul Quinn -- jumping up and down. Only then did I realize I had just won a new car, a 1995 Dodge Intrepid.

Wow, I thought, perfect timing. My old Nissan had 131,000 miles on it, so winning new car was just what I needed. The rest of the round was a blur. A 12-handicapper at the time, I double-bogeyed the next two holes and finished with an 88.

Somebody called my employer, the New York Post, and when I approached the 18th green, I spotted one of our photographers, Wilbur Funches. I spent the next half hour posing for photos with tournament officials. I posed for one picture with the actress Dina Merrill, who was in Caddyshack 2 and also had played in the outing.

The post-golf reception had an open bar, so I didn't have to buy any drinks. Talk about good luck. Later that night, I went to work and had to write a first-person account about my day. I also spent some time on the phone talking with family and friends.

A week later, I got a call from some insurance company. I was told the woman who was supposed to be watching the hole was on a bathroom break when I got my ace, so I was asked if I wouldn't mind taking a lie-detector test. Why not? The idea intrigued me. I had six witnesses who saw it, so I agreed to do it for the fun of it.

About a month later, I drove to some office building in Danbury, where I was hooked up to a machine with a bunch of wires. The gentleman running the machine started out with a bunch of easy questions before he came to the big one I knew was coming. "Did you sneak around and plant the ball in the hole?" All I could do was laugh before I gave my answer — a resounding "no."

I guess I passed the test because I got the car. In late August, three months after I hit the shot, I was told to go the Dodge dealer in Stamford and pick out my car. I got to choose the color, model and any options I wanted. The final bill for my new "forest green" Intrepid was $22,476, which worked out OK for me because the insurance company had given me a $22,000 allowance.

Of course, months later, I learned that $22,000 would be tacked on to my income-tax bill. Big deal. As a result, I paid the government an additional $6,000 for a new car.

NEW YORK POST, **SPORTS** TUESDAY, MAY 16, 1995

'Intrepid' editor hits hole-in-one

By RALPH WIMBISH
Special Projects Editor

I hit the golf lottery yesterday. It was a 44,000-1 shot, a low-rising six iron that was good enough to win a spanking new automobile worth $22,000.

It happened yesterday on the ninth hole at Quaker Ridge Country Club in Scarsdale, where I was playing in the NutraSweet Classic, a charity benefit in behalf of the Juvenile Diabetes Foundation.

According to *Golf Digest*, the odds of making a hole-in-one are about to 44,000-1. Yesterday, I beat those odds. It wasn't my first ace. Five years ago, I used the same club

to ace the 160-yard 15th at Yale.

The ball, a Titleist DT, hit the green and began rolling uphill toward the cup and suddenly disappeared. I turned to one of my playing partners and said, "Did that do what I thought it just did?"

Somebody yelled, "That's in the hole!" Thinking it might have slipped off the back, I ran full speed to the green for verification. Sure enough, there it was.

My playing partners — John Groesbeck, John Tracy, Vincent Sweeney and Paul Quinn — told me it was the car hole. I went wild.

Two hours later, after my 88th stroke, I felt like I had won the U.S. Open. I left the course to a chorus of congratulations, and next thing I knew there were four photographers taking my picture standing next to my new Dodge Intrepid.

Yeah, this hole-in-one was real special. And, best of all, thanks to an open bar, I didn't have to buy drinks for anybody.

OUR ACE IN THE HOLE: *Post editor Ralph Wimbish poses with brand new Dodge Intrepid he won yesterday at Quaker Ridge Country Club in Scarsdale by virtue of scoring hole-in-one during benefit for Juvenile Diabetes Foundation.*

New York Post: W.A. Funches Jr.

Ralph Wimbish's first-person account of his hole-one in 1995 as it appeared in the New York Post.

Strange fact: Six months after my ace, Chris Gargano, my college roommate, won a car with a hole-in-one at a pro-am event in Sarasota, Florida. Chris' ace came just minutes before Hall of Famer Al Kaline aced the same hole. Chris, who was paired with Phil Niekro, had to donate his car back to charity. I got to keep mine.

The Intrepid still ranks No. 1 on my list of cars I have owned. Far ahead of the 1973 Pinto that nearly drove me into bankruptcy. I drove my hole-in-one car for about 10 years. Early on, I would bring it out only for special occasions, like trips to upscale golf courses. Eventually it became my everyday car after my Nissan Sentra died on the Major Deegan one night in 1999.

In 2006, after 120,000 miles, I donated the Intrepid to charity -- the Juvenile Diabetes Foundation, of course.

As for my ball I used that day – my Magic Ball -- that's another story. I got a wooden pedestal and placed it on my porch for all to see. About a year later, I got a chance to play Quaker Ridge again for the Walker Cup media day, so I brought my Magic Ball with me.

When I got to the ninth hole, I took it out of my bag and pulled a 7-iron. This time the hole was playing about 150 yards. I hit a good shot and my Magic Ball ended up about a foot away from the cup. My witnesses that day were Hank Gola, Brian Moran and Tom Meeks, the USGA official.

After I tapped in for birdie, I put the Magic Ball back in my bag, took it home, and returned it to its perch on the porch. It sat there for about a year until the day Frank Paterno, my housemate, brought home a dog that belonged to his girlfriend.

The dog, having no sense of golfing history, saw nothing but a round ball to play with and chewed it up almost beyond recognition.

I almost cried when discovered my Magic Ball in its mangled state. Oh, well!

CHAPTER 29

John Shippen

A long time ago, before there was Teddy Rhodes, Charlie Sifford, Lee Elder and Tiger Woods, there was a gentleman named John Shippen Jr., the forgotten legend of Shinnecock Hills Golf Club.

Shippen not only helped build the course at Shinnecock, he became America's first Black golf professional when he played in the second U.S. Open in 1896 – and nearly won it. Before the tournament started, Shippen's announced participation caused such a stir, a group of golfers threatened not to play until they were told that he was "half-Indian."

But make no mistake, Shippen considered himself a Black man -- and he loved the game of golf. Shippen was born in 1879 in Washington, D.C., the son of a Presbyterian minister who moved his family in 1890 to the eastern end of Long Island to open a church on the Shinnecock reservation. His mother was Shinnecock Native American.

When John Jr. was 12, a wealthy group of Southampton residents forked over $2,500 for some land just north of Long Island's Highway 27. The group, with Shippen's help, designed and built a 12-hole golf course that was expanded to 18 holes four years later under the direction of Willie Dunn.

Dunn, a Scotsman who finished second to Horace Rawlins in the first U.S. Open at Newport in 1895, took a liking to Shippen, eventually making him assistant pro. Shippen gave lessons, repaired clubs and ran tournaments. As a player, club members urged him to compete when it was announced that Shinnecock would host the second annual Open. So, he entered the tournament, along with his buddy, a Shinnecock native named Curtis Bunn.

Theodore F. Havenmayer, the first USGA president, was confronted before the tournament by a group of players – mostly pros from England and Scotland – who threatened to withdraw if Shippen were allowed to play. Remarkably, Havenmayer pacified the protestors, allegedly convincing them that Shippen was half-Black and half-Shinnecock.

The 36-hole event was held at Shinnecock Hills on July 18 with a field of 32. In the morning round, Shippen was paired with Charles Blair Macdonald, the blue-blooded, egomaniacal amateur champion and architect who is considered the father of American golf.

Shippen shot a 78 in the first round and was tied for second place. Macdonald had an 83 and was so disgusted with himself he withdrew from the tournament. Macdonald it is said was impressed with Shippen's play and walked the course with him in the second round.

A report in the Chicago Tribune praised the "16-year-old colored caddie" from Shinnecock. "Anyone who plays Shippen has to forget his boyishness, and pay careful attention to his golf, for Shippen is, in view of the circumstances, the most remarkable player in the United States," the report said.

In the afternoon round, Shippen met doom at the par-4 13th hole after hitting a drive right into a sand pit by the edge of the road. Without a sand wedge, which had yet to be invented, Shippen struggled to advance the ball and carded an 11 on the hole. He finished with an 81 and won $25 for taking fifth place, seven shots behind the winner, Scotland's James Foulis.

Years later, Shippen lamented his bad luck in a magazine article. "It was a little, easy par-4," he said in 1968. "I've wished a hundred times I could have played [it] again. It sure would have been something to win that day."

Shippen played in four more U.S. Opens – in 1899, 1900, 1902 and 1913. In 1902 Open, he finished in fifth place at Garden City, 11 shots behind the winner, Scotland's Laurie Auchterlonie. No other African American played in the U.S. Open until Teddy Rhodes in 1948.

Shippen was later hired as the first head professional at the Maidstone Club in East Hampton, married twice and fathered six children. He also made and sold his own line of golf clubs.

Eventually, Shippen moved to New Jersey, where he lived out his life working at the Shady Rest Golf and Country Club in Scotch Plains. On May 20 1968, he died in near-obscurity at the age of 88.

The PGA of America didn't allow memberships to Blacks until 1961 when Charlie Sifford was allowed to play. Shippen was granted post-humous membership to the PGA in 2009, a true forgotten pioneer of the game he loved.

CHAPTER 30

Charlie Sifford

When I think of Charlie Sifford, I see a man who is the patron saint of African American golfers, a man who should be canonized for his love of a game that didn't want him.

Charlie was not the best golfer in the world, but he certainly has my vote for being the most courageous. It was this courage, dignity and class he showed throughout his career – particularly during the days when Black players were not welcomed on golf courses – that I admire most.

He did this while enduring verbal abuse, hatred, and death threats. Yes, death threats.

It went beyond being told he could not play on a golf course nor participate in tournaments because of his skin color.

As I grew up in the 1960s, my dad told me about Charlie and his struggle to play in PGA tournaments. My dad, an avid golfer, could sympathize, being that he, too, had been turned away from several local public courses. To his credit, my dad fought back. He was persistent, often angry. When he was told he couldn't play, he stubbornly would come back the next day, and sometimes the day after that.

And he took some of those golf courses, notably a new county-owned course called Airco, to court and, with the help of St. Petersburg Times reporter Sam Adams, made sure those lawsuits were well publicized. By 1964, my dad had earned his tee times.

Charlie, who died in 2015, earned his playing time a bit differently. Born in Charlotte, North Carolina, in 1922 (the same year as my dad), he began caddying at age 13 and started playing golf for money when he was 17 years old.

In 1948, Charlie began playing professionally and won the United Golf Association's National Negro Open six times, including five straight titles starting in 1952. He acquired the nickname "Little Horse" from bandleader Billy Eckstine, who hired Charlie as his valet and personal golf coach.

Charlie spent his winters touring with Eckstine and his summers dominating the UGA, though he had a greater ambition.

"I didn't want to beat Black people at golf. I wanted to beat the white people at golf," Charlie would often say.

Charlie used an invitation obtained by heavyweight boxing champ Joe Louis and attempted to qualify for the 1952 Phoenix Open, one of the few events in which Black golfers were allowed to play. When Charlie got to the first green, he found human excrement in the cup. On at least one occasion, his ball was kicked into the rough just as he was serenaded with boos and chants that included the N-word.

In 1955, Charlie shot a career-best 63 to take the first-round lead in the Canadian Open, a tournament that was eventually won by Arnold Palmer. In 1957, Charlie won the Long Beach Open, which was a 54-hole event and not sanctioned by the PGA. At age 34, he beat many of the game's top players like Tommy Bolt, Gene Littler, Gay Brewer and Jack Fleck, all of whom would win major championships.

Charlie did receive encouragement from Jackie Robinson, who in 1959 wrote a column in the New York Post critical of the PGA's discriminatory policies.

"(Jackie) asked me if I was a quitter and I told him no," Charlie recalled. "He said, 'If you're not a quitter you're probably going to experience some things that will make you want to quit. You can go out there and take one of those golf clubs and slap someone up side their head, but you better take it and go about your business.' I promised him I would."

In 1961 under increasing pressure, the PGA did away with its "Caucasian only" rule, opening the door for Charlie to become the first African American to have a tour card. He played in the Greensboro Open that year and finished fourth despite a plethora of racial slurs and death threats.

"If I hadn't acted like a professional when they sent me out, if I did something crazy, there would never be any Blacks playing," Charlie said in 2000. "I toughed it out. I'm proud of it.

"I just wanted to prove that a Black man could play golf."

Chomping on his ever-present cigar, Charlie won the Greater Hartford Open in 1967. But even after his victory in the 1969 Los Angeles Open, he never received an invitation to play in the Masters. Cliff Roberts, the chairman of Augusta National, insisted Black golfers were banned from his tournament because "to make an exception would be practicing discrimination in reverse."

Lee Elder broke the color barrier at Augusta in 1975, and I got to know him and Charlie in 1985 when I worked at Golf Digest. I became quite friendly with Lee, who instantly became one of my heroes in 1968 when he lost a five-hole, sudden-death playoff against Jack Nicklaus at Firestone.

Lee was nice enough to do a number of promotional clinics and TV spots that I arranged for The Commemorative, a senior tour event that Golf Digest held in Newport, Rhode Island. He won that tournament in 1985, beating five-time British Open champion Peter Thomson with an eagle on the first playoff hole. After his victory, Lee invited me to his celebration dinner that night. We were sitting near the bar when I asked Lee if anybody had ever written a book about Charlie.

"Not that I know of," Lee told me. "You should ask him."

Charlie Sifford and Ralph Wimbish at the 2008 Met Golf Writers dinner

I thought about it for a day or two, but I never did ask Charlie. In my mind, I didn't think I had the maturity and mental fortitude to write such a book, a decision I now regret.

In 1992, when I saw Charlie's autobiography, "Just Let Me Play" had been published, I was kicking myself. So, five years later, when I was asked me to do a book about New York Yankee great Elston Howard - another Black pioneer - I didn't hesitate.

Charlie played in 422 tour events and made 399 cuts. He enjoyed a good second career on the senior (Champions) tour and was inducted into the World Golf Hall of Fame in 2004. Two years later, he received an honorary doctorate degree from the University of St. Andrews in Scotland and, years later, he was awarded the Presidential Medal of Freedom.

With all that in mind, I was determined to get Charlie honored at the annual Met Golf Writers Association National Awards Dinner. As an executive MGWA board member, I argued long and hard that Charlie deserved to be awarded the Gold Tee, which has been given annually to golf's greats since 1952 in a ceremony that was the highlight of the dinner.

Fellow board member Dave Anderson, my friend and New York Times sports columnist, backed me up, noting the Met Golf Writers had honored Cliff Roberts with that same award in 1974.

"If we gave the Gold Tee to Cliff Roberts, I'd think it's only right that we give one to Charlie," he said.

And so, on June 23, 2008, Charlie Sifford, at the age of 76, was given the Gold Tee, an award that had been given the likes of Palmer, Nicklaus and Sam Snead.

Gary Player, the 1973 Gold Tee winner, not only presented the award to Charlie that night but also delivered a stirring speech that brought the packed room of 600 to its feet at its conclusion.

"Charlie, when I think of you, I think of a warrior," Player said, addressing Sifford. "You've been a role model for persistence and hard work."

Turning to the audience, Player continued: "He handled adversity with great dignity. Some people thought he was mean, but I'd say you can't blame him if you went through what he went through."

After Charlie got his award, he came over to me, looked me dead in the eye and said, "You should have done my book."

I was somewhat shocked. I guess Lee Elder must have told him about my inquiry all those years ago. I could only shake my head as I told Charlie that he was one of the reasons I wrote the Elston Howard book. Then Charlie surprisingly told me he was not happy with his autobiography. "It wasn't that good," he said. "(The co-author) left out a lot of stuff."

Charlie then asked me to work with him on a new autobiography.

Again, I reluctantly turned down the opportunity. Part of my reasoning this time was financial. I got only a few dollars for all the work I did on the Howard book. Also, I didn't see the need to rewrite something that was already published.

Looking back, maybe I should have tried.

Sorry, Charlie.

CHAPTER 31

Walter Hagen's ghost

Let's go live to the Red Course at Long Island's Eisenhower Park, where the ghost of Walter Hagen is holding a press conference:

Reporter: Mr. Hagen, the Long Island Classic is moving to Eisenhower Park this summer. Is it true it's the only senior tour, er, Champions Tour event left in the New York metropolitan area?

Hagen: Yes, I believe so. It's the same tournament that was played at the Meadow Brook Club for the past 15 years.

TV guy: Walter, you have won two U.S. Opens, four British Opens and five PGA Championships. Is this the same course where you won your fourth PGA title?

Hagen: That's correct, sir, though it was called Salisbury Golf Club back in 1926 when I defeated Leo Diegel in the match-play final.

Radio guy: Does the course look any different?

Hagen: At 6,750 yards (par-70), it's a little bit longer than when I played it. Obviously, superintendent Gene Contino and his staff have put a lot of work into the greens, tee boxes and bunkers. It's a nice public course.

Gossip columnist: Who do you think might win this year's Long Island Classic?

Hagen: Well, it should be a shootout. Expected to play are defending champ Hubert Green, Bruce Fleisher, Lee Trevino, and that Fuzzy guy. Also, there's that chap they call the Walrus.

Food reporter: Craig Stadler?

Hagen: Yeah -- him, too.

Business reporter: What are the tournament dates?

Hagen: Practice rounds start August 11 with the first round set for August 15. Ticket proceeds benefit Schneider Children's Hospital.

Movie critic: Did you see that "Bagger Vance" movie?"

Hagen: Yeah, it was a real stinker. That Animal House guy who played me never got a date with Charlize Theron. Even worse, I didn't win the match.

CHAPTER 32

Gene Borek

With a heart of gold and a swing to match, Gene Borek was a true gentleman of golf, a great teacher and a man of wisdom when it came to discussing the mechanics of life as well as the golf swing.

The longtime head professional at Metropolis Golf Club in White Plains died in 2009, but he will always be long remembered as a local hero among the golf community of metropolitan New York. The consummate club professional, Gene played in 36 major championships and at one time held scoring records at nine golf courses.

Gene perhaps is best remembered for the day he shot an Oakmont course-record 6-under-par 65 in the second round of the 1973 U.S. Open at Oakmont. His "dream round" was also the lowest U.S. Open score in 20 years. He held that distinction for just two days until Johnny Miller clinched the championship with his iconic 63, making Gene the "Roger Maris of Oakmont."

Gene was playing in the seventh of his 10 U.S. Opens when he shot the 65 after opening the tournament with a 77. Hoping just to make the cut, he played a bogey-free round. He holed out from a sand trap to make par and sank six birdie putts en route to the course record at Oakmont, arguably one of the world's toughest golf courses.

"It was one of those rounds you dream about," Gene told me in 2002. "I lit it up in every way. I drove the ball well. The U.S. Open is about hitting the ball straight – you hit the ball straight, you should do well. But getting on the greens is one thing; putting is another."

Gary Player was atop the leaderboard after the second round, followed by the names of Jim Colbert, Jack Nicklaus, Miller, Bob Charles and Borek, who was at even par and tied with Arnold Palmer, Lee Trevino and Tom Weiskopf.

By Sunday, the greens of Oakmont took their revenge and his putter paid the price. Gene shot rounds of 80 and 75 leaving him in 38th place.

As great as Gene's 65 was, it was just another highlight in his amazing career. In his prime, Gene was the Sam Snead of Met-area golf, a section that always has been home to some of the best golfers in the country. Gene's accomplishments remain staggering: Three Met PGA titles, twice Met Player of the Year, three Long Island PGAs, two Long Island Opens and two Westchester PGAs. Twice he was National PGA Stroke-Play champion.

Along the way, he was inducted into the Westchester Hall of Fame and the Met PGA Hall of Fame, received the Horton Smith Award for his contributions to golf education; and was bestowed the title of Master PGA Professional.

"When Gene entered a tournament, he was the man to beat," said Tom Nieporte, the longtime head pro at Winged Foot. "I was playing there at Oakmont when they flashed his 65 on the leaderboard. That was something to see because I knew how tough Oakmont was."

Gene was born in 1936 and grew up in Yonkers, the youngest of eight children. His parents, Anthony and Karen, came to the United States from Warsaw. The family lived near Dunwoodie Golf Course, back then a private club where Gene became fascinated with the game. He caddied, delivered newspapers, set pins at the local bowling alley and spent time on a delivery truck, all to help out at home.

Ralph Wimbish with Gene Borek and Dave Anderson at the Met Golf Writers dinner in 2008.

In his spare time, he played golf, often taking the trolley down to the Bronx to play at Mosholu. He was good enough to captain the golf team at Saunders High School.

In 1954, Gene met a kid named Jon Voight. He was the son of Elmer "Whitey" Voight, the legendary head pro at Sunningdale Golf Club in Scarsdale. Gene beat out Jon that year for the Westchester Caddie Championship and they both went to Columbus, Ohio, for the national championship, where Gene finished third.

"Jon was real good, a scratch player at 17 and 18, with one of the finest swings you ever saw," Gene said. "But Jon got into acting, and that was it for him."

Gene headed to college at Oswego State in the fall of 1954 with the intention of becoming an industrial-arts teacher. But golf got in the way and Willie Goggin, the head pro at Upper Montclair Country Club in New Jersey, gave Gene a job in his pro shop. By the summer of 1955, Gene was working as an assistant for Elmer Voight at Sunningdale.

"(Elmer) took me in and treated me like a son," said Gene, who worked at Sunningdale for eight years. "He said we would be equal partners. He took me down to St. Croix and I spent five winters there with him and got on the Caribbean tour. It was a great experience."

Guiro Cribari, the dean of Westchester sportswriters (and the man who hired me at the White Plains Reporter Dispatch in 1974), said Gene and Elmer were inseparable.

"Unquestionably, Elmer Voight was the quintessential club professional," Guido told me. "His whole life was dedicated to that. What an impressive man; always exquisitely attired. A picture of splendor. Very dapper. Never without a shirt and tie, even if it was 102 degrees. Perfectly synchronized. Always. I remember the day he died (in 1973), in a car accident, in his wife's arms."

Tragically, the crash that killed Elmer Voight came just a few days after Gene had shot the 65 at Oakmont. With his wife Barbara driving, Elmer was in the passenger seat when another car lost its brakes and crashed into the Voights' car on Central Avenue, a busy thoroughfare not far from Sunningdale. Gene was in Chicago playing in the Western Open that day. He immediately pulled out of the tournament and rushed home for the funeral.

Though still playing occasionally on the tour, Gene followed in Elmer's footsteps and became a head professional at the age of 26. Pine Hollow, a club on Long Island, hired him away from Elmer on November 22, 1963, the same day Jack Kennedy went to Dallas. Gene spent 11 years at Pine Hollow.

In 1965, Gene won the first of his three Long Island PGA titles. When he won it again in 1969, his caddie was a young man named Charlie Robson.

"I was impressed how good he was," said Robson, who, with Gene's help, rose from the caddie ranks to become the longtime executive director of the Met PGA.

"Gene had tremendous playing ability. He was a great long-iron player, a good driver of the ball. When he was at the top of his game, I would say he was one of the 100 best players in the United States."

Over the years, Gene was a major force in the growth and success of the Met PGA.

"He could have become president if he wanted," Robson said, "but Gene always enjoyed being in the background. He's not one to stand in front of a podium."

In 1972, Gene tied for 29th place at the PGA Championship. In 1974, he again changed jobs, leaving Pine Hollow to succeed Jack Grout (on his way to join Nicklaus at Muirfield Village) at La Gorce Country Club in Miami Beach. But one year later, the head job at Sunningdale was his for the taking, and Gene brought his family back to New York.

Curiously, Gene never became a touring pro. Sure, he thought about it, but he told me he never felt comfortable being away from his wife Joan and their four kids.

"You've got to be motivated to be a touring pro," said Carl Lohren, Gene's longtime friend and himself an esteemed teaching professional.

"I didn't think Gene was ever motivated in that way. He grew up poor in Yonkers and had made something of himself. He was happy where he was."

Lohren met Gene in 1964 when they were neighbors in Long Island. Gene became one of the "professors" at Lohren's golf school and co-starred prominently in both of Lohren's instruction videos, the first entitled "One Move To Better Golf."

In the fall of 1966, Lohren said he "stumbled" on the method he called "one move."

"Starting the swing with the left shoulder is the key move," Gene explained. "It begins the windup of the body. It has to turn sooner than later. It's very much Hogan-like."

Personally, I became a better golfer because Gene taught me the "one move." In 2006, after I had somehow injured my hip, I went to see Gene to fix my golf swing. He was fighting off cancer as he was winding up his 25-year tenure at Metropolis. Yet he often took time to fix my golf swing. I offered to pay him for the lessons, but he wouldn't have it. So, I repaid him by "loaning" him some old photographs and some golf instruction books that I knew he would treasure. I also presented him with a mock back page of the New York Post that pictured him under the words GENE-IUS.

"The game was in his DNA and he was filled with anecdotes and stories," said Les Schupak, a past president of the Met Golf Association. "He knew the rules as well as any golf pro who played the game. He was the consummate professional."

Gene's not around anymore, but when my golf swing needs tuning up, I can always crank up my VCR, watch the "One Move" video and say "thank you" to one of the nicest human beings I ever met.

CHAPTER 33

Arnie Palmer

Nobody knew U.S. Open heartbreak quite like Arnold Palmer. "The King" played in 32 Opens but only once did he emerge victorious.

Palmer finished in the top ten 13 times; five times as the runner-up. In one five-year span (1962-66) he lost three 18-hole playoffs.

Only Phil Mickelson can come close to matching Palmer's U.S. Open record of frustration. Going into 2021, Phil had played in 29 U.S. Opens with no titles and six second-place finishes.

Palmer, with a little luck and a better putter, might have won the U.S. Open five or six times to go along with his six other major championships.

In 2009, I wrote a story for the New York Post's pre-tournament package when they played the U.S. Open at Bethpage Black in Farmingdale, New York, and got to ask Arnie to list his "most memorable" U.S. Opens. Here they are, beginning with his lone U.S. Open victory followed by the losses he remembers most -- in order of frustration:

1960 (Cherry Hills) -- "I think it's pretty why it's pretty obvious why it's No. 1 on my list," said Arnie, who was seven shots back starting the final round. He began his charge by driving the green on his first hole and making a two-putt birdie en route to a 65 that enabled him to hold off 47-year-old Ben Hogan and a 20-year-old amateur named Jack Nicklaus.

1962 (Oakmont) -- Despite three-putting 11 greens, Arnie, the "hometown favorite," could have won the championship with a 10-foot birdie putt on the 72nd hole. The putt didn't drop, leaving Palmer to face "Fat Boy" Nicklaus the next day in an 18-hole playoff. "Are there any good putters in the crowd?" Arnie asked his army the next day after losing the playoff to Jack by three shots.

1973 (Oakmont) -- "It must have been a good day for the grass to grow," Arnie moaned, "because I left a whole lot of putts short." During the final round, Arnie was tied for the lead but missed a four-foot birdie putt on 11 and bogeyed three straight holes starting at 12. He tied for fourth behind Johnny Miller, who started the round six shots off the pace and won with a record-setting 63. John Schlee finished second; Tom Weiskopf was third; and Palmer finished in fourth place tied with Nicklaus and Lee Trevino.

1966 (Olympic Club) -- "I've spent four decades trying to explain what happened," said Arnie, who led Billy Casper by seven shots with nine holes to play. But Palmer stumbled home with a 39, needing a six-footer for par on the 72nd hole to finish off a 71. He made the putt, but Casper shot a 32 on the back nine, forcing Palmer into another 18-hole playoff. The next day, Arnie was up by two shots with eight holes to play but gave back six shots and lost to Casper by four.

1963 (The Country Club) -- "Frankly, it hurt like hell," Arnie said of his second straight loss in an 18-hole U.S. Open playoff. Arnie's low point? He missed a two-foot putt on the 71st hole and finished tied with Julius Boros and Jackie Cupit. In the "A-B-C playoff," Palmer needed three hacks to escape from a tree stump on the 11th hole and finished six shots behind the sweet-swinging Boros.

1967 (Baltusrol) -- "Jack was a different animal altogether, completely unlike anyone I'd ever chased," said Arnie, who went head-to-head with the Golden Bear and again came in second, four shots back. On the final day, they started dead even, but Jack birdied five of six holes starting at the third hole and never looked back in winning his second of four U.S. Open titles. Palmer's 69 was good enough to make him the second non-winning player in U.S. Open history to break 280.

1972 (Pebble Beach) -- "It got to be ridiculous," Arnie said of his putting. In the final round, he missed an 8-foot birdie putt at 14 that could have given him the lead. He bogeyed the next two holes and closed with a 4-over 76 to finish in third place as Nicklaus won the third of his four U.S. Open titles.

1974 (Winged Foot) -- Arnie shared the 36-hole lead with Gary Player, Ray Floyd, and Hale Irwin at 3-over. In the third round, Palmer shot a 73 and trailed the leader, Tom Watson, by two shots. On Sunday, Arnie three-putted the second green from 12 feet en route to a 76 and fifth place, five shots behind Irwin, who won the "Massacre at Winged Foot" with a score of at 287, 7-over par.

For Arnie, it was his final top-five finish in a major championship.

Palmer, who died in 2016 at the age of 87, won 62 PGA tournaments; 11 international tournaments; 10 Champions (Senior) Tour titles between 1980-88; and nine other non-PGA tournaments. Six of his seven major championships came in a five-year (1960-64) span.

He was "The King."

CHAPTER 34

Ralph Hutchison

There! Right there! That's him!

He's the man on your TV set in the bright red blazer and a white Panama hat, roaming around the 18th green at Augusta National. Yeah, check out those old highlight films on Golf Channel and you can't miss seeing Ralph Hutchison.

He was the man with the booming voice who called out the scores of Arnie, Sam, Jack and others on the final hole of just about every major golf tournament from the late 1940s till the mid-1970s.

"I started announcing in 1948," Hutchison told me in 1975 after he worked the 18th green at the Westchester Classic, which I was covering for The Reporter-Dispatch. "That's what I became known for, not my golf."

Hutchison, born in 1908 in Pawnee, Oklahoma, was once an accomplished golf pro. He toured the country with Ben Hogan and Jack Grout and played in the first of his six U.S. Opens in 1934. He tied for eighth in the 1945 PGA when it was match play and was 41st in the 1946 Masters. In 1954, he won the Philadelphia Open and another tournament in Jamaica.

Ralph Hutchison and his booming voice for years were a fixture at Augusta National's 18th green.
Courtesy Augusta National

"I learned the game of golf from Macdonald Smith," said Hutchison, recalling his association with one of golf's top players back in the hickory-shaft era.

Hutchison, a former quarterback at Southern Cal, got his first golfing job in 1931 as an assistant to Tommy Armour, the legendary "Silver Scot" who began his tenure in 1925 as the head pro at the Boca Raton Club.

Soon after, Hutchison was hired as one of the first assistant pros at Augusta National, a job he held for three years starting in 1932. In

1935, Ralph's great-uncle, Hall of Famer Jock Hutchison, played in the first of his 12 Masters. From 1963-1972, Jock was one of the original honorary starters.

Ralph eventually landed in eastern Pennsylvania, where he was hired in 1935 as the head professional at Saucon Valley, the prestigious golf club that was run by E.G. Grace, the president of Bethlehem Steel.

One year during the late '40s, while working at Saucon Valley, Hutchison entered the Los Angeles Open and was among the leaders after two rounds when he got a call from Grace's secretary. She told him Mr. Grace was heading to Aiken, South Carolina, and he expected his golf pro to be there to play a round at nearby Augusta National.

Ralph had no choice. He immediately left Los Angeles and flew to Aiken. But they never got to play because it rained like the dickens for several days.

"I would be playing in a tournament and would drop out because I was playing badly or some other reason, and that's when I began to announce scores," Hutchison recalled. "I learned my style from Scottie Chisolm, the Scotsman who founded the Los Angeles Open."

In 1948, a sore wrist forced him out of the Masters, and that's when he came up with a novel idea.

"Bobby Jones, Cliff Roberts and I were standing around the 18th, and it dawned on me that the only way those people out there would know the scores would be to go up to the player and ask him," Ralph recalled.

Back then, there was no TV or leaderboards. Ralph said he then suggested to Jones that someone should be announcing the scores to the crowd at the 18th green.

"Mr. Jones told me to 'go get a green coat and get down there and tell those people what's happening.' A half hour later, I was standing on the green announcing," Ralph said.

Sandy Hutchison, Ralph's son, said his dad recommended having announcers on the ninth and 18th greens.

"He said they should be PGA of America members, so they'd know the rules and the players would know them and feel comfortable," Sandy said in a 2012 interview.

After the players putted out, Ralph would announce what they shot for that day and for the tournament. He was also on the rules and the pairings committees.

"He enjoyed being a tournament official," Sandy said. "It was more than just being the announcer."

No microphone or megaphone was needed. Ralph had a voice that could be heard in the next county, and he soon became a colorful fixture on the 18th green at most of the major tournaments this side of the Atlantic.

Hutchison was also a teaching pro. In 1975, he told me he had 23 PGA Tour pros and six LPGA players in his stable, though he refused to name names. He also became a historian and collector of prized memorabilia, including sets of hickory-shafted clubs owned by the likes of Harry Vardon and Bobby Jones.

Jack Nicklaus is said to have called him, "my second favorite teacher," after Jack Grout, Jack's boyhood instructor.

"I never wanted to do anything else in my life but teach and play golf," Ralph told me. "Harry Cooper, Mac Smith and Sam Snead were the best swingers in golf who ever lived. Cooper and Smith could hit all day and never touch the grass. They never took divots. Hitters don't last long in this game, but swingers do."

Ralph worked the 18th green at Augusta for the last time in 1971, when he stepped aside because of throat problems, his son said. Leo Beckmann took his place before giving way in 1998 to Johnny Paulk and later Scott Davenport in 2018.

He did a few other tournaments and ended his announcing career sometime in the mid '70s. He retired from Saucon Valley and moved to Sarasota, Florida, with his wife Ruth.

Ralph died at the age of 85 on April 3, 1993.

Fittingly, it was Masters week.

CHAPTER 35

A Good Walk Spoiled

Here's the book on my old buddy Bob Labbance. He loved golf; he loved the New York Yankees; and he died from Lou Gehrig's disease.

Labbance was living in Vermont in 2008 when he passed away at the age of 55 from amyotrophic lateral sclerosis (ALS), the same disease that claimed the lives of former Yankees Gehrig and Catfish Hunter.

ALS is a progressive neuromuscular disease that weakens and eventually destroys motor neurons. Life expectancy is usually three to five years after diagnosis. According to the ALS Society, the disease affects about 30,000 patients in the United States.

"Hey, at least I have a disease named after a famous Yankee," Bob told me shortly after he got his diagnosis in December of 2007. "Every day I'm on this planet is a great day.

"But the body is breaking down faster than I anticipated. My legs are gone, and I'm having trouble getting my arms over my head, which was not the case just a couple of weeks ago."

*Bob Labbance survived a paralyzing injury in 2004, only to die
from Lou Gehrig's disease four years later.*

I met Bob in 1997 at a golf outing at Winged Foot Golf Club in Mamaroneck. We bonded over golf and the Yankees that day and he invited me to Vermont to play two of his favorite courses. I accepted, of course, and one week later we walked 36 memorable holes -- Green Mountain National in the morning and Neshobe that afternoon.

Bob was editor of several regional golf magazines, and I soon became not only his friend but one of his go-to contributing writers. In 2002, when I got married on Long Island, Bob drove all the way from a Kentucky that day to be there. And he was the first of my friends to greet me that evening at the reception.

But Bob's life took a dramatic turn on August 31, 2004, when he was playing golf at a course in New Hampshire. An avid walker, he had his golf bag on his shoulders when he slipped on a rain-slick footbridge and plunged head-first into a water hazard. His head hit a rock and he floated helplessly face down in the water.

"I knew exactly what had happened," he recalled. "I knew I was seriously injured. I couldn't feel my legs and arms. They were just jangling, vibrating, tingling."

Fortunately for Bob, his longtime friend Kevin Mendik was right there to pull him out of the hazard before he could drown. Kevin phoned for help, and Bob was helicoptered to a nearby hospital.

For days, Bob said he endured "total pain" and the fear of paralysis. Doctors performed surgery to relieve pressure on his spinal cord. The 5 1/2-hour operation was deemed a success, and Bob was soon able to move his legs and knees. A week later, doctors got him to sit up in bed for what Bob later called "the most painful minute of my life."

Despite the excruciating pain, Bob kept sitting up every day. He spent months in a physical rehabilitation center in Colchester, Vermont. As bad as that was, Bob was in more agony that October as he watched the Yankees blow a three-games-to-none lead to the hated Boston Red Sox in the American League Championship Series.

"Talk about pain," he said. "That really hurt."

With hours of therapy and truckloads of unpronounceable medications behind him, Bob made it back to his feet before Christmas. At first, he had some mobility problems on his right side but soon was back in his office writing about golf and visiting courses.

He was an 8-handicapper before the accident but that spring – eight months after the accident -- he was thrilled to hit a tee shot 150 yards.

Slowly, it appeared as if life was returning to normal. But in the spring of 2007, Bob began losing mobility and coordination. New medications and new doctors didn't help. By the fall, he needed a cane and eventually a walker.

That December, Bob went to a hospital in Boston, where he saw a doctor who suspected a motor neuron disease, suggesting it was triggered by a traumatic incident, perhaps a blow to the head.

"It sounded like something fixable," said Bob's wife Kathie. "But then we Googled it when we got home and it led directly to ALS links, a very big 'uh-oh' for us. Needless to say, this was a very scary and depressing situation."

Still, Bob remained upbeat. He worked as hard as he could to finish the last two of the 16 books on golf he wrote — "The Life and Work of Wayne Stiles," an appreciation of the noted golf architect; and "The Vardon Invasion," a perceptive account of golfing great Harry Vardon (1870-1938) and his tour of America in 1900.

By March, Bob had accepted his fate. He knew would never play golf again. He spoke about the tireless love of his friends and family, particularly his two kids, Griffin and Simone, both of whom had been adopted. To be sure they made it through college, Bob established a scholarship fund.

Through it all, one of Bob's last wishes was to attend a Yankee game at Yankee Stadium. He wanted to get to The Bronx for one last look at his team – and field -- of dreams. He never made it.

Until his dying day, however, he considered himself "… the luckiest man on the face of the earth."

CHAPTER 36

Italia 1990

Imagine a job assignment where you are sent to Italy for three weeks to write about the world's greatest sports spectacle. That's just what I got to do when the New York Post sent me to cover the U.S. national soccer team in the 1990 World Cup. A grand adventure it was.

Soccer, or *calcio* as it's known in Italy, is a sport I learned to appreciate when I spent four months in Rome working at the Daily American in 1982. That was the year Italy, behind Paolo Rossi, won the World Cup in Spain. Along with most Italians and my cohorts at work, we watched each game on TV as if it were the seventh game of baseball's World Series. To this day I still consider Italy's 3-2 nerve-wracking win over Brazil in the quarterfinals to be one of the best games I ever witnessed.

And so, eight years later when I was asked to follow Team USA to Italy for the World Cup, I jumped at the chance.

This was to be the USA's first World Cup appearance since 1950 when the Americans stunned England 1-0. Walter Bahr played on that team and would later become the head counselor at Camp Acadia, a

Catholic summer boys camp I attended in 1962 and 1963. He also fathered two sons (Chris and Matt) who were NFL place-kickers.

OK, now I was all set to fulfill my dream of being an overseas correspondent. I got my press credentials and called my travel agent. I also took a crash course from Berlitz in speaking Italian. Unlike 1982, I wanted to be able to carry a conversation – and make sure I could go to any trattoria and fluently order spaghetti carbonara.

Meanwhile, my first taste of American soccer came on May 5 in Piscataway, New Jersey. I went to Rutgers Stadium to see the U.S. play a friendly against Malta. Bob Gansler was the Hungarian-born U.S. coach. He was somewhat optimistic after a 1-0 victory before an enthusiastic pro-U.S. crowd of about 7,000.

We're getting better," Gansler told reporters. "Our formula is simple. Eleven guys play offense, and 11 guys play defense."

Gansler's team was a collection of young, former collegiate all-stars with little international experience. Make no mistake. Tab Ramos, Desmond Armstrong, Tony Meola and their teammates were good all-American types, but there were no Diego Maradonas on this team.

Oddsmakers gave made the U.S. a 500-1 shot to win it all. Brian Glanville, the British sportswriter who would later do a weekly soccer column for The Post, dismissed the U.S. squad as "a galumping side of corn-fed college boys."

Four days later, I drove to Pennsylvania to cover USA's surprising 3-1 win over Poland. The game was played in Hershey, just down the road from where Wilt Chamberlain scored 100 points in one game against the New York Knicks in 1962.

Later, while Team USA began packing its bags for training camp in Switzerland, I was packing my bags for Northern Ireland. Hey, I figured I could get in a few days of golf before heading to Italy, well in time for the USA's World Cup opener in Florence against Czechoslovakia on June 10.

Northern Ireland? I had heard great things about its golf courses --
particularly Portrush and Royal County Down. My friends asked me if
I worried about "all the trouble over there" and my standard reply was
always: "Not really, I work nights in New York City."

So, on Monday, May 28, I arrived in Belfast. My first stop was
Royal Portrush, where I was paired with Father Jim, a Catholic priest
who assured me I had nothing to worry about in Northern Ireland.

"Stick to the golf courses, lad," Father Jim told me en route to my
jet-lagged round of 91. "Stay away from the hot spots (in Belfast) and
you'll be fine."

The next day, Tuesday, I played in the morning at Portstewart before crossing the River Bann for an afternoon round at Castlerock.
There, I was paired with one of the club's members, an older gentleman
who introduced himself as Arnold.

After the round, Arnold invited me up to the clubhouse bar for a
drink. When I ordered a glass of Harp, Arnold waved off the barkeep
and told him, "Give my friend a Smithwick's." Well, that was my first
and some 30 years later I haven't had my last.

As the evening progressed, fellow members arrived at the bar and
Arnold introduced me to each of them as "my sportswriter friend
from New York who's going to Italy for the World Cup." And with
each introduction, that member would buy me a shot of Bushmill
Whiskey.

Needless to say, by 10 p.m. or so, I was in no condition to drive
anywhere, so Arnold insisted I take a room at the "Golf Hotel" right
across the street. Arnold not only paid for my room, he and one of his
buddies carried my luggage up the stairs before bidding me farewell for
the night.

Van Morrison was another reason why I went to Northern Ireland.
He had just released an album, Avalon Sunset, that contained a lushly
produced, spoken-word song called "Coney Island." On my way from
Portrush to play Royal County Down, I drove to the scenic seaside

town to see if it had a Ferris wheel and roller coaster like its Brooklyn namesake. I am glad to report it did not.

By Friday, June 1, I was back in Belfast to board a plane to Milan. Before setting off to join the U.S team in Switzerland, I checked in with my office in New York and learned that Bucky Dent just had been fired as Yankees manager.

Crossing the Swiss border in my rental car, I spent the night in Lugano, overlooking scenic Lake Lugano, before heading three hours up the road, through the Alps, toward St. Gallen, where the U.S. team had scheduled a tuneup against Switzerland's national team.

That day, I saw the U.S. team's ego take a hit, the result of a 2-1 loss to a mediocre European side that had not qualified for the World Cup since 1966. Bruce Murray's goal gave the Americans a 1-0 lead in the 22nd minute, but the Swiss stepped up on the gas in the second half and Gansler's team definitely looked gassed.

"Pressure is the key word," Gansler told a gaggle of American reporters. "What you cannot do, and what we did, is forget our aggressive mentality."

I was able to chase down Uli Stielike, the German-born Swiss coach, who told me the U.S. team lacked physical dominance.

"It can be a problem to play every three days a very hard game," he told me in broken English. "I don't know if they're prepared to do that. We have to see."

By Monday, Team USA had returned to Italy and set up camp in Tirrenia, a small town on the Mediterranean coast, about 45 miles outside of Florence. The team worked out at an athletic complex that I must say was extremely well-guarded. Dozens of military police surrounded the field, easily spotted with the Uzis they cradled in their arms.

Gansler said his team had no problem adjusting to the fortress-like military atmosphere. "We played all our qualifying games in Central America," he said.

Gansler was in a good mood that day, even when pressed by an Italian writer who wanted to know if his players were abstaining from sex like Italy's coach, Azeglio Vicini, had asked his team to do before the World Cup.

"I have read about those tests about how sex affects performance," Gansler said, "and they are inconclusive."

Asked if his any players on his team were permitted to leave training camp to socialize with the local *signorini*, Gansler chuckled and said, "Next question."

The Italian writer was not amused by Gansler's answer. "He thought it was a joke," he said. "I was serious."

Sunday, June 10 arrived and with it came the U.S. World Cup opener against the Czechs. The mood that afternoon at Florence's Community Stadium was quite sobering, mainly because alcohol sales had been banned for 24 hours.

The noisiest disturbance occurred before the game when members of the Mount Vernon (New York) Soccer Club led a red, white and blue parade of vocal, flag-toting American fans around the stadium.

"American fans don't cause trouble," said a security official named Alessandro Sauli, who assured me 500 police had made Community Stadium the safest place in town.

Every American in the crowd of 33,266 and every player on the field stood proudly at the playing of the "Star Spangled Banner" before kickoff. It felt good to be an American on the World Cup stage. Unfortunately, it was the high point of the day for Team USA.

The best thing the Americans can say about their humbling 5-1 loss was that they were able to score a goal against a technically superior Czechoslovakian squad. I wrote in my lead that it felt like the neighborhood bully had beaten them up and taken their lunch money.

"Obviously our inexperience showed," Gansler told reporters after the game. "We started out with confidence but we gave up a couple of soft goals. We didn't give a good exhibition of what we could do."

After filing my stories, I got a taxi and asked the driver to take me to the best pizza place in town. And I am happy to report that I was able to conduct an entire conversation with my driver in Italian. Those Berlitz lessons were paying off. I got my pizza and a beer (alcohol was now available) before returning to my tiny motel room on the outskirts of town.

The Americans still had two more matches — Italy on June 14 and Austria on June 19, games they would lose. Meanwhile, I had to get some sleep. I had to be up at 7 a.m. for a flight to Sardinia to cover the England's game against Ireland.

Who knows? Maybe I'd meet a hooligan.

CHAPTER 37

Hooligans!

Just because he looked like a hooligan, Ian Ames told me that was no reason Italian police should treat him "like scum."

Ames was one of the more fashionable 35,238 fans at the Ireland-England World Cup game in June 1990 in Cagliari, Sardinia. He came decked out in a dirty white T-shirt, faded blue gym shorts with a Union Jack about his shoulders and a gold stud in his left ear. His hair was spiked and his breath was ... well, let's just say he needed some mouth-wash -- and a bath.

"Totally awful," Ames growled. "We're being treated like animals."

Ames might have had good reason to be upset. Italian police had been hounding fans like him in anticipation of the hooligan scare that had cast a dark shadow on England's rabid soccer fans.

Fourteen English fans – termed as "animali" by the Italian press -- were arrested in the streets one night earlier in the week, and others had been chased out of local bars and restaurants.

Steven Paul Scarrot, the self-proclaimed "No. 1 hooligan," was ar-rested at Rome's Termini train station. He was apprehended by police when he was found wandering on the train tracks carrying a half-empty, five-liter bottle of wine.

Scarrot had been spotted earlier at the Colosseum, yelling desultory comments to nobody in particular about the Dutch national team and their orange-clad fans.

"I'm the greatest hooligan in the world and they'll never stop me," Scarrot, draped in a Union Jack, barked at TV cameras as the police took him away.

In Cagliari, there was too much security at the stadium for anybody to get arrested. The atmosphere at this 1-1 standoff had the charm of a Mitch Miller singalong inside a detainment camp.

Heavily armed police – sometimes 10 deep -- lined every aisle. English fans were outnumbered as they sang out their cheers from the east end of the stadium, often drowned out by the noise coming from the Irish fans on the west side of the pitch.

Helicopters hovered in the twilight with scores of security forces entrenching the sidelines, some with dogs. At the concession stands, there wasn't a beer to be had except for the Dansk no-alcohol brew imported from Denmark.

Getting inside the stadium was a chore in itself. Marty Williams and Gary Moses came all the way here from Kent to be harassed. Dressed up in dingy shorts and Union Jacks, they were frisked twice before reaching their seats.

"This is disgusting," said Moses, who claimed police had been following him and his grimy-looking pals since they arrived here two days earlier.

"There's no reason for this," he said. "At lunch today, we were pulled out of our rooms and searched for no reason at all. I was laughing and one of the police officers didn't take to it. He pulled his gun and said he'd shoot me if I did it again."

The Irish? The green-clad lads were happy with the 1-1 draw, so happy they did not want to leave the stadium despite the urgent pleas of the PA announcer. They, too, had been searched and scrutinized, but they didn't seem to care.

"The Irish never cause any trouble," said one young fan from Dublin. "We just want to sing our songs and have a good time."

That they did.

CHAPTER 38

Marvelous Marvin

Marvelous Marvin Hagler was in the corner of the U.S. soccer team when it got knocked out by Italy in the first round of 1990 World Cup.

The former undisputed middleweight boxing champion sat quietly in the press box, two rows behind me, in Rome's sold-out Olympic Stadium as we watched Team USA's 1-0 loss to the Italians.

The boxer "nobody wanted to fight" had moved to Italy after his final fight, a controversial 1987 split-decision loss to Sugar Ray Leonard. Hagler agreed to an interview after the match and told me this was the first time he'd ever watched a soccer game.

"They gave it their best," he said. "If enough Americans are watching back home, maybe they'll get some new recruits to do better in 1994."

I asked Hagler, who was then 35 years old, if he wanted a rematch with Leonard.

"I have no plans to fight," he said. "I'm retired from fighting. I'm putting that energy into acting. I'm not going to win an Oscar, but I need a new challenge, and acting seems to be it."

Hagler, whose career record was 65-3-2, had just completed shooting his second movie, a sequel to the 1989 Italian action film entitled Indio. In both movies, he played Jake, a U.S. Marine sergeant who fights a large corporation that wants to destroy the Amazon rain forest.

Hagler also starred in a 1996 science-fiction film called Virtual Weapon.

Hagler, who died in March 2021 at his home in New Hampshire at the age of 66, legally changed his name to include his adopted nickname in 1982 after a ring announcer had failed to introduce him as Marvelous before a fight.

"You know," he told a British newspaper in 2019, "one time, Joe Frazier told me that there were three things going against me: one, I was Black. Two, I was a southpaw. And three, I was good. "He was right, too … it was never easy."

CHAPTER 39

Maradona's last hurrah

June 21, 1994 — After 83 glorious minutes, Diego Armando Maradona was finished for the day.

He shook the hand of American referee Arturo Angeles, handed over his captain's armband to teammate Oscar Ruggeri, and proudly accepted a standing ovation from the pro-Argentina crowd of 53,586 in Foxborough, Massachusetts.

It seemed as if it were old times for the pudgy, 33-year-old megastar, who returned to the World Cup stage with flashes of brilliance, scoring the third goal in the 60th minute of a 4-0 World Cup victory over Greece.

Since his last appearance in the 1990 Cup in Italy, Maradona had battled weight-gain issues, feuded with the press and police, was accused of alcohol abuse, lost a paternity lawsuit and was busted for drug use and banned from Japan.

On this day, however, all was forgiven when the 5-foot-5 artful dodger split two defenders and sent a booming shot from 15 yards out high into the left corner of the net.

"I'm letting my actions speak for themselves," Maradona told the media in Spanish. "I dedicate my performance to them, the critics who said I couldn't play anymore. I'd like to see what they now have to say."

Starting at midfield on the right flank, Maradona was immediate prey for Greek defenders who tried desperately to keep him from igniting Argentina's downfield attack.

Maradona was fouled five times in the first half, mostly by Panagiotis Tsalouchidis. The Greek defender was yellow-carded in the 24th minute for a hard foul on Maradona and also was whistled for pulling on Maradona's shirt 14 minutes later.

Playing in his fourth World Cup, Maradona didn't appear to be as out of shape as he reportedly was a month earlier. He looked right at home as he fed the ball to his big guns, Claudio Caniggia and Gabriel Batistuta, who scored Argentina's other three goals.

The Greek coach, Alkis Panagoulis, said his team played in fear. "We came to take a picture of Argentina and Maradona," he said. "I never thought my players would be so afraid."

In the 59th minute, Maradona broke free at midfield and charged downfield before he passed off to Caniggia on the right wing. Seconds later, after a corner kick, Maradona was free in the middle when he took a pass from Fernando Redondo and scored with a hard shot off his left foot.

It was his first World Cup goal since he scored in the 1986 semifinals against Belgium. Argentina won the Cup that year as Maradona scored five goals, including his controversial "Hand of God" score – where the officials did not see him illegally palm the ball into the net -- that helped beat England in the quarterfinals.

Years later, he fessed up. "It wasn't the Hand of God," he said in 2002. "It was the hand of Diego."

On this day, Maradona celebrated his ninth World Cup goal by dashing into the left corner and screaming at the TV cameras as he was being mobbed by teammates.

No "Hand of God" this time. Just applause.

———————

As it turned out, this was Maradona's last goal for Argentina. A week after this game, he failed a drug test and was sent home, ending an international playing career that saw him score 34 goals in 91 games. Sadly, he died in November 2020 at the age of 60.

CHAPTER 40

Italy vs. Ireland

It was hot. It had sizzle. It was Ireland versus Italy in a 1994 World Cup matchup at Giants Stadium. I was there on June 18, one day after the infamous O.J. Simpson car chase, to write about it for the New York Post when it dawned on me that this was much, much more than a soccer game.

It was a pint of Guinness against a bottle of Peroni. A shot of Jameson versus a glass of Chianti. Maureen O'Hara against Sophia Loren. Bono against Pavarotti. Danny Boy against Rigoletto.

There was color: The greens against the Azzurri. Red, white, and gold flags flapping in the breeze. Red, white, and green banners waving back.

And then there were the songs: Ireland's green-clad fans cheering their heroes with "We Are the Boys in Green." Italy's fans chanting bits and pieces from "Aida."

Food? It was boiled potatoes against ravioli. Corned beef against pizza. Custard against cannolis. Irish coffee against cappuccino. Soda bread vs. Panettone.

Ireland had a goaltender named Packie Bonner. Italy had Roberto Baggio, a practicing Buddhist with a ponytail. Ireland's best defender was named Phil McGrath, the namesake of a fine Irish ale. Italy had a flamboyant striker named Giuseppe Signori, whose nickname was "Beppe."

This was Erin Go Bragh versus Forza Italia. The Saint Fin Barre's Cathedral against the Sistine Chapel. St. Patrick against St. Francis of Assisi. Jerry Quarry against Nino Benvenuti. The Liffey River versus L'Arno.

Odds were 25-1 for Ireland to win the Cup. Italy's odds were 6-1. Ireland was coached by an Englishman, Jack Charlton. Italy's coach, Arrigo Sacchi, was a former shoes salesman.

It was Killanarney against Spoletto. Dublin against Rome. Cork versus Naples. The Chieftains against Tony Bennett. The Quiet Man versus The Godfather.

Ireland's top players competed in England's Premier League. Italy's best players competed in Serie A of the Italian League.

This was James Joyce versus Leonardo Di Vinci. Aer Lingus against Alitalia. The Irish Echo against Oggi. Bensonhurst against Woodside. The shamrock versus garlic. The Blarney Stone against Mount Vesuvius.

At game's end, the scoreboard read Ireland 1, Italy 0. Ray Houghton scored the only goal in the 12th minute when he intercepted an errant Franco Baresi header just outside the Italian penalty box, cut to his left and arched a left-footed shot over the head of a stunned Gianluca Pagliuca and into the net.

"Just dipped it over the keeper's head," said Houghton, a stubby native of Scotland who qualified to play for Ireland because of his dad's Irish ancestry.

Sacchi, the Italian commissario technico, said his team "didn't deserve to lose."

"I didn't see a disaster out there today," he said via an interpreter. "We didn't play our best game today. We must do better."

As both squads left the field, two green-clad Irish fans dashed onto the pitch and were immediately tackled and arrested by New Jersey state police.

"Those boys who ran on the field were from New York," Charlton explained between puffs of his victory cigar. "Irish fans don't do that."

Charlton's lads had scored Ireland's first-ever World Cup victory, but it was all for naught. A 2-1 loss to Mexico and a scoreless draw with Norway got them into the Round of 16, where they were eliminated by the Dutch, 2-0.

As for Italy, the Azzurri made it to the final match. They rebounded with a 1-0 win over Norway and a 1-1 draw with Mexico to reach the knockout stage, where they scored consecutive 2-1 wins over Nigeria, Spain and Bulgaria. However, they lost the final to the boys from Brazil 3-2 on penalty kicks.

Oh, well. That's amore.

CHAPTER 41

Ali, Sinatra and Mr. T

Boxing may not be my favorite sport, but it remains one of the most memorable. Memorable because of particular events that involved Muhammad Ali, Frank Sinatra and the actor we all know as Mr. T.

Let's start with Ali, or shall we say Cassius Clay, as he was known as in 1964. My dad took time off from his busy schedule on February 25 so he could go to Miami Beach and attend Clay's heavyweight title fight against Sonny Liston.

I couldn't go. I was 11 years old and it was a school night. However, my mother allowed me to stay up past my 9 o'clock bedtime and we turned on the radio. After each round, the radio host would tell us who won the round and describe the action from wire reports. Like Liston's previous fights with Floyd Patterson, we anticipated Clay wouldn't survive the first round. Boy, were we wrong.

To our surprise and joy, Liston didn't answer the bell for the seventh round. Clay was the heavyweight champion.

Fast forward to May 25, 1965. It was another school night for me, but I begged my dad to take me to see the rematch on closed-circuit

TV over in Tampa at Curtis Hixon Hall. To my delight, my dad said OK and my mother didn't object.

"This is going to be a great," I told myself as my dad and I settled down in our seats. The fight began — and it was over just like that. Ali KO'd Liston with a phantom punch. I started yelling, "Get up," not because I was rooting for Liston, but because I wanted to see a fight. Meanwhile, the guys behind me began yelling "Fix!" and that was that. Everybody went home shocked. I'm surprised there wasn't a riot.

A few years later, in 1976, Ali had a big title fight against Ken Norton at Yankee Stadium. As a member of the media, I was able to get a seat in the fourth row at the Westchester County Center for the closed-circuit broadcast. Oddly enough, the first three rows were roped off and I soon found out why.

Just before the opening bell, Frank Sinatra and his entourage burst through the side door and took their seats directly in front of me. As I watched the fight, I thought to myself I could get an exclusive interview with Old Blue Eyes. Hey, he was sitting two rows up, right in front of me.

When the fight ended, Sinatra and his troupe didn't hang around to hear the decision. As they made a beeline to the side door, I followed in hot pursuit, notebook and pen in hand. Sinatra got to his limo and I was about six feet away when suddenly an arm the size of a hamhock came flying across my chest.

"Uh, my name is Ralph Wimbish, and I'm a reporter. I'd like to interview Mr. Sinatra," I said.

"Not tonight," replied the burly gentleman who had stopped me. I'm sure he was a bodyguard.

Oh well, I returned to the arena and was surprised to hear Ali was awarded the decision though it appeared he had been outclassed by Norton, the guy who had broken Ali's jaw in 1973.

About a month later, I attended a testimonial dinner for Tony Janiro, a boxer I had never heard of. At the time, he had just turned 50 and was tending bar in The Bronx.

That night, a bunch of his buddies got up to the podium to praise Tony, whose record was 83 wins, 11 loses and two draws. They told stories about how he grew up in Youngstown, Ohio, and worked his way up to become "main event fighter."

"I fought Rocky Graziano back in 1950 and '51, just before he became middleweight champ," Tony told me.

In three fights against Graziano, Tony lost twice and gained a draw. He also told me that he fought Jake LaMotta but didn't say anything about it.

OK, four years later, I'm in a movie theater watching Raging Bull and I almost dropped my popcorn when I saw Tony's name come on the screen. I must say Kevin Mahon, the actor who played Tony, took quite a beating after LaMotta's wife, played by Cathy Moriarty, had enraged Jake (played by Robert DeNiro) by telling him that Janiro looked "handsome."

Fourteen years later, in 1990, I finally attended my first live boxing event. I was in Las Vegas, where Iran Barkley was challenging British boxer Nigel Benn for the middleweight title.

The fight was nationally televised on a Saturday and held at Bally's. I entered the ballroom but did not go immediately to my seat. I wanted to scope out the scene. So there I was standing next to a side door when suddenly it burst open and there was Mr. T, with his Mohawk and tons of gold jewelry around his neck.

Mr. T entered the room, looked directly at me and barked, "How's it going, brother?"

I was dumbfounded, shocked. I didn't know what to say. I think my reply sounded like Jackie Gleason's "humina, humina, humina."

Mr. T seemed to laugh and proceeded to his ringside seat, where he sat next to Petula Clark, Redd Foxx and Gene Hackman.

I took my seat just before the opening bell. The fight was a real slugfest. It took 20 seconds before Benn sent Barkley crashing to the canvas, but he got up and hit Benn with a couple of good shots before Benn knocked him down again. Barkley got up but Benn decked him again just before the bell sounded. Barkley looked dazed but not hurt, yet the referee stopped the fight, invoking the three-knockdown rule and awarding the fight to Benn.

Like the Liston-Ali fight, there was booing and cries of "fixed" from the audience. Once again, I felt like I was cheated from watching a good fight.

Oh well, at least this time I can say I got to see Mr. T.

CHAPTER 42

Dartmouth's finest

Way back in 1970, when Hair was hummin' on Broadway and Streisand was singing her heart out, Ed Marinaro was crooning the Hill Street Blues after he and his team ran into the buzzsaw that was Dartmouth College's football team.

Marinaro, the College Hall of Fame running back from Cornell, was one of my first phone calls when Dartmouth Alumni Magazine asked me to do a cover story about its school's unbeaten 1970 team.

"They were the last great Ivy League team," Marinaro told me in 2010. "They could have played with anyone in the country. Dartmouth was that good."

Yep, Coach Bob Blackman was the maestro of this masterpiece. His Green Machine went 9-0 that year and was ranked as the 14th best team in the country – ahead of perennial powers Southern Cal and Oklahoma -- according to two wire-service polls.

Dartmouth also won the Lambert Trophy, an honor that has been bestowed to the best team in the East since 1936. That 1970 team was clearly the best of Blackman's 16-year reign at Dartmouth, where he compiled a 104-37-3 record.

Blackman's team never trailed in any game that season and out-scored its opponents, 311-42. His defense was so dominant that it posted six shutouts, including four straight to end the season.

It's not surprising some experts say Blackman's team, led by 26 talented seniors, was the greatest team in Dartmouth's fabled football history. Seventeen players on that team received All-Ivy League recognition and five were named All-East.

To each of his players Blackman was like a Nat King Cole song — unforgettable in every way.

"Coach Blackman made it possible for us to execute at the highest level possible," said Murry Bowden, the Texas-born co-captain and College Hall of Fame linebacker. "I'm the guy in the Hall of Fame, but I wouldn't be there without my teammates. We had lots of characters on our team, a fantastic, spirited group of personalities, but everybody loved each other. We knew how to win."

Blackman was labeled "an Ivy League Lombardi" by Sports Illustrated. He was a barrel-chested mound of manhood with the mind of a genius. His distinctive, authoritative voice was at times down-right frightening, especially when amplified by his trusty bullhorn. In a sweatshirt at practice he looked like Bill Belichick; at games in his best suit he resembled Hank Stram, his dapper figure always topped off with a fedora.

"He was a gentleman, and that's what I remember most," said co-captain Bob Peters, an All-Ivy defensive tackle who described himself as one of Blackman's "unruly" players.

"I didn't appreciate his good example at the time," Peters said. "But after graduating from Dartmouth I came to realize what a rare human being he was. On one hand he was diligent, persistent and tough. But on the other hand, he attempted to show appreciation for each of his players."

"Bullet Bob" prowled the sidelines with a limp, the result of a battle with polio in 1937 when Blackman was a freshman football player at Southern Cal. He was given little chance to walk again, but one year later he was back on the football field as an assistant coach. After the war he became a head coach: first at the San Diego Naval Academy, then Pasadena City College and eventually Denver University.

In 1955, when DeOrmond "Tuss" McLaughry was fired after a fifth straight losing season, Dartmouth turned to Paul Brown, the legendary NFL coach, for help. Brown, whose son Mike (Class of '57) had played quarterback at Dartmouth, formed a search committee that eventually recommended Blackman for the job.

Few coaches ever had Blackman's passion for the game. Every player received a daily mimeographed sheet with timetables and charts, each one detaining exactly what he was to do when on the field. And each of Blackman's drills was timed to the minute.

"Sometimes he was a pain in the ass," said Bob Cordy, a former offensive guard who became a Massachusetts Supreme Court judge. "I liked him, but he wanted 110 percent. He'd say, 'This is the game and how it is to be played. If you want to win, this is how it's supposed to be done.'"

Blackman is said to be one of the first college coaches to use computers to track tendencies of opponents. Said Bowden, "He didn't hesitate to scout other teams, and we would pick up certain tendencies and formations they would like to run in certain circumstances."

When it came to offensive play-calling, Blackman was the Lex Luthor of his day. He was one of the first coaches to use the V formation in the offensive backfield, an early precursor to the wishbone. And he was notorious for diabolical offensive schemes that featured plenty of reverses and lateral passes. To avoid penalties, Blackman often went to the referees before the game to warn them about any trick plays he might use that day.

"He was obsessed, an organized genius," says Dan Radakovich, an offensive lineman. "He was the most organized person I ever knew. He broke it down so you could know your function, and it all fell into place. If it wasn't perfect, it wasn't good enough for him. Every aspect of the game -- from the way we dressed, lined up, played, everything -- had a purpose."

Murry Bowden was an All-American linebacker for Dartmouth's unbeaten football team in 1970.
Courtesy of Dartmouth College Athletics

Blackman, who coached Dartmouth's undefeated teams in 1962 and 1965, realized there was something special about the freshman class of 1967. More than 100 students -- that's about one out of every five in the class -- tried out for the freshman team that year, back in the days when first-year students were excluded from the varsity.

Socially diverse, they came to New Hampshire from places such as Snyder, Texas; Glendale, Arizona; and Bozeman, Montana. They came when the times were a-changin' all across America. With the Vietnam War and civil-rights battles ongoing, there was turmoil everywhere.

Everywhere, that is, except on Blackman's football field.

"There was so much going on somewhat or other, but all we could think about was the next day at practice," said Tom Price, a defensive end turned cardiologist who was one of 10 African Americans on the 1970 roster. "Football allowed us to get away from the times. There were radicals on campus, but no one said football players had to take a stand. We were not politicians."

Maybe the smartest move Blackman ever made at Dartmouth occurred in the 1968 season, when he played many of his sophomores throughout a 4-5 season, giving them the added experience they would later need to put Dartmouth back atop the Ivy League.

In 1969, Dartmouth went 8-1 and won a share of the Ivy League title, but the entire season is remembered by the one game it didn't win — a 35-7 thumping at Princeton.

"I still have nightmares over it," Cordy said. "Blackman panicked. We saw Blackman like we'd never seen him before. He made all these complex changes on the offense and on our approach, and they didn't work. That loss made us miserable and we vowed to make sure it never happened again."

It didn't. In 1970, Blackman's ornery team was ready to go the distance.

"We could be arrogant, we could be nasty, we'd hit Marinaro and tell him not to get up," said Barry Brink, a defensive tackle who, along with Bowden and defensive back Willie Bogan, were known as the Killer Bs of the defense.

Bogan, an academic All-America and Phi Beta Kappa graduate, was so good, he was drafted the following spring by the Baltimore Colts, even though it was known he had accepted a Rhodes scholarship to attend Oxford University.

"Willie was a great player," said Brink. "He had no interceptions his senior year because nobody ever threw at him."

And nobody ran at Bowden. The 5-foot-10, 190-pounder who wore the number 10 was a "rover back" who manned the middle with the vengeance of a rabid Mack truck.

Said Marinaro, "People ask me who hit me the hardest, and I tell them Murry Bowden, and that includes the NFL."

That season Dartmouth's defense ranked in the top 10 nationally in seven categories, including first in scoring defense, second in total defense, third in rushing defense and fifth in pass defense.

Blackman's defense was perfectly complemented by his offense, led by quarterback Jim Chasey, a California beach bum who shared Ivy League Player of the Year honors with Marinaro and went on to play in the Canadian Football League with the Montreal Alouettes.

"I was worried about him," said Jim Risley, a defensive lineman from Arkansas. "He was so laid back; nothing ever bothered him. I guess that's what made him such a good quarterback."

Nicknamed "The Snake," Chasey missed the first game that season with an ankle injury. With Steve Stetson and Bill Pollock filling in, Dartmouth overcame a sluggish start to beat UMass, 27-0.

Chasey returned the following week and led the Green to a 50-14 victory at Holy Cross. Then came Princeton and sweet revenge. The largest crowd (21,416) in Memorial Field's history saw the home team blank the Tigers, 38-0.

"They didn't have a chance," said Radakovich. "We destroyed them. They didn't realize how good we were."

After an easy 42-14 romp over Brown, Blackman notched his 100th win at Dartmouth with a 37-14 victory at Harvard before a crowd more than 35,000. John Short, a workhorse in the backfield, came up big, rushing for 106 yards and two touchdowns, plus he threw a 49-yard option TD pass to Bob Brown.

"They strangled you on defense and didn't let you breathe on offense," said John Yovicsin, Harvard's coach.

Halloween arrived one week later and with it a big showdown at the Yale Bowl in New Haven. A sun-soaked crowd of 60,820, plus a regional TV audience, saw Dartmouth prevail over the nationally ranked Elis in what one writer said was "the most lopsided 10-0 game in the history of Ivy League football." The stat sheet showed Dartmouth with 25 first downs and 480 yards of offense. Yale had 11 first downs and 190 yards of offense. The score was close only because three of Chasey's passes were intercepted in the end zone.

Said Brink, "They were the only team that had a chance to beat us. It was a healthy fear, if you know what I mean. Once we got that game, we knew we could go undefeated."

In the home finale against Columbia, Chasey raced 75 yards for a touchdown in a 55-0 rout. Then it was on to Cornell. That score was 24-0 as Short upstaged Marinaro and rushed for 192 yards. Marinaro, the nation's leading rusher averaging 166 yards per game, managed only 60 yards on 21 carries.

Dartmouth was 8-0 with one game to go. Because the Ivy League didn't allow its teams to accept bowl invitations, the game at Penn was its last hurrah.

Playing before a spirited crowd of 42,328, and on artificial turf for the first time, Dartmouth dominated the Quakers, 28-0. Short ran for 154 yards and Chasey completed 15 of 19 passes for 164 yards. Bowden, named to the All-America team the day before, intercepted three passes.

Blackman was carried off the field. The perfect season was over, and soon after so were Blackman's days at Dartmouth. After he was named Walter Camp Coach of the Year, he packed his bags for Illinois and rode off into the sunset of the Big Ten. In 16 seasons, his record at Dartmouth was 104-37-3.

Before he left Hanover, Blackman laughed off a challenge from Penn State coach Joe Paterno, whose team had finished with a 7-3 record.

"Of course, Coach Paterno knows that under Ivy League rules we're not allowed to play a postseason game," Blackman said. "If we were to play in such a game, we would prefer to play a team that had a better season than Penn State."

———

Blackman coached at Illinois for six seasons, compiling a 29-36-1 record, before returning to the Ivy League in 1977 as Cornell's head coach.

"I like the Ivy League," he said. "It's the only conference where coaches are paid more than the players."

Blackman retired after the 1982 season with a record of 168–112–7 and was inducted into the College Football Hall of Fame as a coach in 1987. He died in 2000 at the age of 81.

CHAPTER 43

Jim Caniano

There was the laugh. The Jim Caniano laugh. When you heard him laugh, you laughed – and you didn't have to know why he was laughing, either.

Yes, the Jim Caniano laugh was that infectious.

Actually, Caniano had two laughs. There was the growly "heh-heh-heh-heh" version as well as that hissy sound he made when he was just trying to be polite or he wanted you to feel good after you had just told a joke that didn't work.

I first heard that laugh in January of 1973 when Jim moved into our dorm, ETA 1, at the University of South Florida after he had transferred from Texas Western, the school now known as UTEP. I had never met anyone from Texas before, but there was something about this Italian kid with the New York accent. Turned out, he was from Dobbs Ferry and his dad owned a big dry-cleaning business in The Bronx.

We soon become good friends – and rivals. Jim, you see, was quite an athlete. He teamed up with Richard Bass and, against me and Chris Gargano, became our fiercest stickball opponents. Jim was also a crafty basketball player when we played those 11 p.m. pickup games over at the Andros courts. And somehow, he became the manager of our dorm softball team. I can still hear his "go get 'em" speech before a game where we got our butts kicked by a score of 29-10.

A year later, when we decided to have an election for softball coach, I was Jim's campaign manager. His slogan was "Tippecanoe and Caniano, Too!" He lost the election, but he didn't quit the team. He was our center fielder as our team made it to the campus semifinals.

Earlier that year, when our dorm decided to have a mock homecoming dance, Jim headed the panel to pick our homecoming queen. The lovely Alecia Berman was the winner, and guess who got to be her escort? "Heh-heh-heh-heh."

Sure, Jim dated some nice girls. There was Michelle, then Nancy, and others. Yet, somehow he never married. Part of his bachelor mystique, though, we learned later that he had a secret pact to marry one of his financial clients, Bonnie, if both of them were still single somewhere down the road.

Jim graduated from USF in 1975 with an accounting degree and took a job at Busch Gardens. Along the way, he cemented friendships with the likes of Knute Gursky, Buzz Coren and, of course, Jim Montante. The two of them became roommates who knew how to have a good time. "Heh-heh-heh-heh."

In 1981, Jim teamed up with Buzz to put together the first of our two dorm reunions at the Holiday Inn in Tampa on Bearss Avenue. I'm sure anyone who attended remembers how well it was organized. And, well, we all had a great time just being there. "Heh-heh-heh-heh."

By 1990, Jim had become a reputable businessman with the founding of Precision Business Services in Largo. When it came time to do my taxes, your taxes, anybody's taxes, he was a real pro.

In 1991, Jim and I started taking our late-December golf trips to Myrtle Beach. For 10 years straight, we would rent a condo or two and invite a number of our buddies to play golf. That's when he met Paul Campbell and, eventually, it became an annual Ryder Cup-like event we called the Advil Cup.

Jim Caniano was in the wedding party when Grace and Ralph Wimbish got married in 2002.

In 1998, Campbell convinced Jim, Moe Mitterling, Frank Paterno, Bill Stieg and myself to come to Michigan for a week of golf at Crystal Lake. That's when Jim began his famous barbecue dinners. For whatever reason, he went all out — ribs, pulled pork, shrimp cocktails. His dinners were so good, we eventually named our annual summer golf trip in his honor.

As of 2021, 23 years later, we are proudly known as Friends of Caniano United, aka FOCU. "Heh-heh-heh-heh."

But Jim stopped coming on those trips in 2017. We knew he was battling Crohn's disease and some other stomach issues; we just didn't how bad it was. He wouldn't tell us.

There are dozens of Caniano stories I can tell you about this man. The baseball and football games he loved to attend. The concerts we got to see. A week spent driving down the coast in California in 1993, stopping off at Big Sur to hit golf balls into the Pacific. Later that night, we arrived at our friend's apartment complex near L.A. and the security guard called our buddy to say, "two Mexican guys are looking for you."

There was a golf trip to Ireland in 2000. Intense games of air hockey. The time he and Jim Melvin tipped over their canoe at Crystal Lake. Even the night a bunch of us went to a restaurant called Brewmasters and got chased out by the waitress who falsely claimed we didn't tip her. "Heh-heh-heh-heh."

This is how we rode with Jim Caniano – when he laughed, we laughed.

Except for Christmas Day in 2018, the day we found out he had died. The laughter was no more. Just tears.

Acknowledgements

With no sports to watch on TV due to the corona virus pandemic, I went into my attic and dug up my collection of newspaper clippings. There, on those yellowed papers, from published stories to travel diary entries, I found 40 years of my life. It didn't take me long to realize I had enough material to do a career retrospective and beyond.

To help weed through this behemoth collection, I brought in Bob Decker. I worked five years with Bob when he was sports editor at the New York Post and he was a good man to work for. Thanks to Bob, I got to design the back page, analyze NFL games, cover the 1990 World Cup in Italy and two Masters as well as write a weekly column on rotisserie baseball. His friendship, advice and editing were invaluable to putting this book together. Thanks, Deck!

Also, special thanks goes out to Phil Mushnick, Bill White, Arlene Howard, Boyzell Hosey, Ann Brandon, Nancy Benson, Chris Gargano, Dave Blezow, Lisa Furlong, Hank Gola, Marty Appel, Marino Parascenzo, Pete Zapadka, Adam Henig, Kevin Mendik, Peter Botte, Charlie Robson, John Steinbreder, Peter Golenbock, David Guo, Doc Giffin, Moe Mitterling, Rob Hooker, Angelo Spagnolo, Jean Schob, Greg Gallo, Bruce Smith, Clay Swenson, Rick Carpiniello, Chuck

Stogel, Mike Vaccaro, Mike Taylor and Carol Capobianco. And to all the unmentioned assists, you know I am grateful to you, too.

I would also like to thank my wife, Grace, for her love and support. For years, she suggested (she might say begged) me to put pen to paper and share my stories. I wouldn't have taken those first steps without her gentle (sometimes not so gentle) inspiration to sit down and get this book done. I love you, Sweets.

Lastly, I'd like to thank my parents. I learned to love sports and the value of integrity as a kid growing up in St. Petersburg. Guided by their love and wisdom, Ralph and Bette Wimbish were the finest of people and the greatest of parents. I am one lucky guy.

— Ralph Wimbish

About the author

Ralph Wimbish was an editor and writer for 25 years in the New York Post sports department. In 2001, he co-wrote with Arlene Howard "Elston And Me: The Story Of The First Black Yankee." In 2017, he co-authored "Throw The Ball High," the autobiography of famed college basketball referee Mickey Crowley.

Ralph is a native of St. Petersburg, Florida, and a graduate of the University of South Florida. He and his wife Grace reside in Calabash, North Carolina.

CPSIA information can be obtained
at www.ICGtesting.com
Printed in the USA
LVHW081542280421
685859LV00021B/222

9 781649 907264